PRAISE FOR SUSTAINING EXCELLENCE

In the modern world of education, it seems as though everyone is writing a book. Everyone is grabbing a microphone. Everyone is dropping nuggets of recycled wisdom, but this is different. For years I have had the opportunity to hear Marty speak, share his stories, and inspire me to be real, because that's what he is. Real! This book is filled with truth and practical application.

Marty moves beyond telling us what we need to do to by also providing the strategies to actually do it. From hiring staff to fit into our "family" dynamic to building a culture that sustains, Marty walks us through his story to help us create the school futures we desire.

I have been waiting to read this book for years, and I am so glad it is finally here!

Dave Schmittou
Author, Coach, Consultant, Leader, Learner

Marty Silverman has been a leader in the educational circle for over 40 years. His wisdom & approach to education has influenced generations of leaders. His book shares tried and true strategies that build upon campus culture & climate. The book contains many of the secrets as to why his school had limited vacancies & numerous applicants every year. This book is a must read!

Todd Bloomer
Principal, Author

Martin Silverman's *Sustaining Excellence: How Culture Drives Teacher Retention* is an insightful exploration of the critical role school culture plays in keeping great teachers. Silverman outlines practical strategies for leaders to create positive, supportive environments where teachers thrive and remain committed. From fostering school "families" to giving teachers meaningful autonomy, each chapter is filled with actionable advice backed by real-world examples. Particularly in an era of teacher shortages, this book is a timely guide for those looking to build a strong, lasting school community that values its educators.

Dr. Chris Galloway
Education Executive Coach & Veteran Superintendent

◆

As any words of wisdom from Marty Silverman promise to be most meaningful and helpful, *Sustaining Excellence* is a book filled with innumerable gems for all educators no matter the role or level of experience. While it is undeniable that teacher retention is an ongoing issue, Marty projects a posture of hope and optimism. Interweaving authentic experiences from educators in the field along with his own stories adds to the narrative structure that makes the book seem like personalized, intimate advice. Marty's brilliance from years of experience is amplified in the book and what results is a blueprint for maintaining a place where the adults who care for the kids are inspired, nurtured, and cared for so they keep coming back.

Michelle Papa
Principal

◆

In *Sustaining Excellence*, Martin Silverman highlights the critical role of creating a family-like atmosphere in schools. He demonstrates how schools can thrive by fostering genuine connections and trust among educators, emphasizing that a supportive culture is key to teacher retention. Silverman also explores the importance of a "yes" culture, where flexibility, a growth mindset, and the courage to let go of rigid structures empowers teachers. This book is a must-read for leaders aiming to create nurturing environments where teachers and students alike can flourish.

Daniel Martinez
Principal

In his book, author Martin Silverman explores the profound impact that a positive school culture has on teacher retention. Through compelling anecdotes, his personal experiences, and perspectives from people in the field, Silverman illustrates how supportive environments foster collaboration, professional growth, and a sense of belonging among educators. What sets this book apart is its actionable insights. Silverman provides practical strategies for school leaders to cultivate a thriving culture that not only attracts but also retains passionate educators. It is a testament to the idea that when teachers feel valued and supported, they are more likely to stay, thrive, and ultimately make a lasting impact on their students.

Michelle Allen
Principal

If there is one aspect of educational leadership Martin Silverman knows well, it is the importance of a having a healthy school culture and climate. Having worked with Marty for many years, it is evident to me that he not only understands this concept, but more importantly, knows how to move a campus towards reaching this goal in a tangible way. Filled with relatable content and actionable strategies, this book is certain to be a valuable resource for administrators and those in school leadership positions for years to come.

Dan St. Romain
Educational Consultant

Martin Silverman's *Sustaining Excellence* is a must-read for school leaders who want to build a thriving, teacher-centered culture. With a clear and engaging style, Silverman offers practical strategies and inspiring stories that demonstrate how schools can create a supportive and empowering environment where teachers can thrive. This book is a roadmap to building a school where excellence is not just a goal, but a way of life.

Joshua Stamper
Author, Speaker,
Director of Innovation, Teach Better Team

◆

Sustaining Excellence is a strong read for any administrator, especially those who are seeking to either revamp, rebrand or rebound within their school. The central focus on lenses that allow for the hiring of staff members who can fit within the desired school culture, or a "family," presents leaders with a shift in hiring mindsets.

With this new mindset, it is easier to see the process of building families within a school setting. Those who read this novel, will be challenged to think beyond technical skills and focus on building a campus culture around staff capacity to collectively work toward student success. Excellent read, thought provoking and heart warming at the same time.

Donald Stewart
Assistant Superintendent of Teaching and Learning

◆

Martin Silverman's *Sustaining Excellence* offers a practical guide for school leaders focused on building sustainable teams through teacher autonomy and a culture of openness. As a veteran superintendent, I appreciate Silverman's emphasis on empowering teachers to innovate, which enhances retention and fosters creativity. The step-by-step process for creating trust, allowing staff to try new ideas, and addressing failures aligns with what I've seen in successful schools. *Sustaining Excellence* provides the tools leaders need to cultivate a positive, lasting culture where teachers feel valued and empowered.

Joe Sanfelippo, PhD
Retired Superintendent, Author, Speaker

Impressive! In light of the current challenges related to retaining teachers, Martin has effectively highlighted the factors educators value and what leaders can influence: culture. He organizes his book as a guide with practical steps and real-life examples, drawing from his own experiences and including authentic voices from the field to underscore the importance of fostering a culture that encourages retention. Martin emphasizes fostering adaptability and autonomy and recognizing educators' diverse needs. This is a must-read that offers valuable perspective and resonates with many.

Dr. Monica Anguiano
Leadership Consultant, Innovative Staffing and Talent Pipelines

---

Martin Silverman's *Sustaining Excellence: How Culture Drives Teacher Retention* offers an essential blueprint for building a positive, family-like school culture that fosters teacher retention. Silverman emphasizes the importance of creating an environment where teachers feel valued, supported, and connected, treating them as individuals with unique needs. His step-by-step guides are practical and easy to implement, making this book accessible and actionable for school leaders at any level. Passionate and grounded in experience, Silverman's focus on empathy, open communication, and personalized support creates a roadmap for fostering teacher success and long-term retention.

Melissa Williamson, Ed.D
CTP, CEO

Marty's years and wisdom as a school leader are evident as this book serves as a roadmap for school leaders who are ready to take meaningful steps toward creating a better environment for their staff. It acknowledges the external challenges but empowers leaders to focus on what they can control: the daily actions and decisions that shape school culture. In doing so, schools can create an environment where teachers want to stay and where they can build long, fulfilling careers. The time to act is now, and this book provides the tools to make that happen.

Kevin Curtis
Educational Consultant

◆

When I heard through the "Campus Leader Grapevine" that Marty Silverman was writing a book, I immediately said out loud, "FINALLY!" Which is my abbreviated way of saying, "Finally, we have a real school leader writing a real book with real insights and real strategies about what it really takes to be an effective leader in education." Once I dug into the pages, I found exactly what I expected: An honest, practical, straightforward guide for building campus culture that works for everyone - educators, kids, parents, and the community. While more money is being spent today than ever before on trying to solve the teacher retention puzzle, Marty spells out the precise solution for the price of a paperback book.

Hal Bowman
Author, Speaker

◆

Improving culture is something none of us perfect. But having a roadmap to improve upon and grow your culture is necessary. That's why I love Martin's book so much! It's such a great roadmap that every stakeholder could find value in! I'll be coming back to this book again and again.

Todd Nesloney
Author, Speaker,
Director of Culture & Strategic Leadership at TEPSA

SUSTAINING EXCELLENCE

How Culture Drives Teacher Retention

Martin Silverman

Sustaining Excellence: How Culture Drives Teacher Retention

Copyright © by Martin Silverman
First Edition 2024

All rights reserved.

No part of this publication may be reproduced in any form, or by any means, electronic or mechanical, including photocopying, recording, or any information browsing, storage or retrieval system, without permission in writing from the publisher.

Road to Awesome, LLC.

To Brenda for putting up with my nonsense for all these years. Your sacrifice does not go unnoticed. You've listened to my stories, laughed with me, and you reminded me often that it was all going to be OK. And you were always right!

To my adorable children, Elena, Evan, and Easton and their spouses (Andy, Saphire, and Barbara) for being great practice in learning to be an effective educator and father. But mostly for producing my exquisite grandkids. Tell them that Papa loves them.

To the memory of my exceptional mentor, C. Michelle Barrera, who taught me how to see both the big picture and the small details. She also taught me how to prioritize relationships while creating an engaging, positive, and high-achieving school culture. Most importantly, she taught me it was OK to cuss at school… sometimes a lot.

To all the educators, students, and families I had the privilege of serving with: You were seen, valued, and heard.

TABLE OF CONTENTS

Foreword	1
Introduction	5
Chapter 1 Schools Need to Create Families	11
Chapter 2 Teachers Need Real, Appropriate Autonomy	39
Chapter 3 Manage Workload by Mastering the Calendar	61
Chapter 4 Creating a Culture of "Yes"	83
Chapter 5 One Size Does Not Fit All	105
Chapter 6 Make Room for Real-Life Stuff	133
Conclusion	157
Acknowledgements	161
About the Author	165

FOREWORD
by Brian T. Miller
Principal, Montana

Do you ever have those days, where a word said or someone's actions are so frustrating or shocking that you just play it in your mind, over and over again? To the point that you talk to yourself in the hallways or lose focus on simple tasks and conversations?

I have those days. And as a principal, they come from all angles. Sometimes, it's an email from a frustrated parent. Other times, it's an interaction with a teacher or a conversation with the district office. And even other times, it is just me and my head, wrestling through something, unable to find clarity or relief.

Normally, I hate these kinds of days. But in the past few years, I have come to appreciate them, if only because they draw me to Mr. Silverman.

It is often said that leadership is lonely. And it is. Or rather, it can be. As a building leader it can be difficult - if not impossible - to find deep and open relationships with those who call you, "boss." But that doesn't mean leadership is lonely. We just have to get creative, think outside the box, or, as it was for me, start calling a retired elementary principal from beautiful San Antonio, Texas. I started doing so a few years ago and have never felt lonely since.

"Got a second?" I will ask or text. And the answer is always, "Yes." Then, for the next thirty minutes or so, I chat Mr. Silverman's ears off, unloading my frustrations or questions.

What I get in return is a calm voice, smooth and simple advice, and 40+ years of educational wisdom. What I get is clarity and the confidence to move forward. What I get is Mr. Silverman.

And Mr. Silverman is as real and practical as they come.

Like you, I don't have time for games and gimmicks. And I certainly don't need more empty promises that read smoothly on a page or sound good from a stage. What I do have time for are actionable ideas that can be used tomorrow. What I do need are solutions that have been tried and tested in real schools with real people.

And that is exactly what Sustaining Excellence provides, tangible ideas from a credible source, that can be implemented instantly.

As educators, we understand we cannot do this alone, that we need help and support, and that we need sustainability. The problem, for me anyway, is that we get so distracted and overwhelmed with current needs and crises that we are unable to spend the appropriate time planning for sustainability. Sustaining Excellence does this for us. It provides simple strategies that have resounding impacts on our culture now, and in the future.

But it is also so much more.

Sustaining Excellence is also an opportunity to sit with Mr. Silverman, hear his words, and connect with his stories. It is a chance to rest in his wisdom and experience of excellence and sincerity that can be difficult to find.

Reading Sustaining Excellence is an investment into your school, an aid to your profession, and a cup of coffee to your educational soul. Because of Mr. Silverman.

"My friends call me Marty," Mr. Silverman recently told me on the phone, but I just can't seem to do it. It's too informal, too relaxed, and I admire him way too much. After reading Sustaining Excellence I might have to change, and not because my admiration has lessened, but because it has grown, has deepened, I have also come to fully understand that sincere connection is at the core of all that Mr. Silverman does and that relationships are the heartbeat of who he is. After reading Sustaining Excellence, you will see this as well.

Sustaining Excellence offers more than just practical advice for the educational leader – it's a reminder of the power of mentorship, human connection, and relationships that fuel our professional and personal growth. Marty's wisdom shines through every page, not only as a guide to improving schools but as an invitation to reflect on the importance of genuine support systems. Through his stories and strategies, you will find clarity, confidence, and a renewed sense of purpose. It's a must-read for anyone seeking sustainable success in education with a heart.

INTRODUCTION
The Time to Act is Now

When I became a first grade teacher almost 40 years ago, schools were very different and yet very much the same as they are today. Students were assembled into age-level groups, the curriculum was organized in skill sets, students attended from morning to afternoon, we walked in lines, we had lunch in the cafeteria, and we played on the playground at recess. There was an expectation that students would progress through content at roughly the same rate. The starting salary I earned for my first teaching job was $16,500 per year. My expectation that first year was that I would do the best job I could for my students and come back the next year prepared to do a better job from the things I learned that first year. And so on, and so on.

Within the past few years, employees were leaving their jobs at an unprecedented rate. The Great Resignation affected many businesses in America, including in the field of education. During turbulent times, any organization must reassess and take a reflective view of how they operate at their essence. This is especially true in organizations that serve the public, and education is even more affected by this phenomenon. Doing the work of schools - the essential work of educating our children while transmitting our culture - demands that we staff our buildings with the finest human capital possible. However, as we maneuver a culture of workers that crave and demand choice, we are tasked with creating a school culture that makes it easy for school staff to stay and build their craft while also building our communities.

Building culture is much like building a strong structure. The foundation and the infrastructure are the most important parts, and yet, they are the least obvious when we admire the finished product. Creating a strong base takes work, but it is essential work. In schools, the functional aspects of the building are secondary to the strength of the human structure. Old-timers will tell us that their schools didn't have the technology, furniture, or creature comforts that new schools possess. It's true that a great teacher can teach in the shade of a tree, and still, teachers often are lured away from schools to the newest, shiny-object schools. Is it the buildings that are luring teachers to new situations?

A more disturbing trend is the number of teachers who leave the education profession entirely. A quick review of educational social media will show you countless stories of teachers who are flat out leaving the profession to work in industry, other service professions, or jobs where their unique skills are valued. We are not, nor will we ever be a work-from-home profession. Education requires personal connections and a physical closeness that can't be effectively replicated online. If we learned anything from the Covid-19 pandemic it was that schools work best when teachers and students are in the same physical space. Teachers leaving the profession cite personal safety and security as high on the list of reasons they leave. But toxic cultures are also high on the list of reasons teachers choose to leave the profession.

There are many things school leaders can do to create a culture that retains teachers. We typically cannot change state and federal mandates such as high-stakes testing, salary scales, union contracts, or political interference, to name a few. What we can control is the way our schools implement policy. The actions you will read in the following chapters will help guide you in your plans to build a culture that accepts mandates and makes them work for the teachers, students, and communities.

This book aims to equip school leaders, teachers, and communities with the tools to create a culture that makes teacher retention the norm rather than the exception. In this book, you will find concepts and ideas that can begin your thinking on how to create a culture that retains great teachers over time. More importantly, you will learn some actions you can implement immediately. While culture builds over time, actions can begin right now. As we navigate the increasing demands of our profession and service to our communities, we cannot wait to act. Let's get on with retaining our teachers!

CHAPTER 1
Schools Need to Create Families
Creating School Families is a Deliberate Act

"I love my work. We have some good times here, and they take care of me. This is my extended family here, and I look forward to coming in each day."
~Dortha Chapman

SCHOOL PERSONNEL DO NOT FEEL CONNECTED TO THEIR SCHOOLS

Look anywhere in the news, social media, or the staff lounge, and you will hear the dire statistics that tell us teachers are leaving their schools, and even the profession, in droves. This is not a new phenomenon. Teachers and other school personnel have been leaving the profession even before the pandemic created more difficult conditions for the education profession. What makes this time in our professional lives even more difficult is the spotlight on teachers and schools in the past couple of years.

According to a report from the Brookings Institute, research on teacher commitment to remaining in the classroom as a result of the Covid-19 pandemic noted the following:

- In March of 2020, the reported probability of teachers leaving their state or profession increased 24% on average.
- By March 2021, it increased to 30%.

A survey by the Rand Corporation (2021) found that:

- Nearly one in four teachers reported they would leave the profession by the end of the 2020-2021 school year and this percentage was higher with black teachers at 50%. This is a large increase from one in six teachers pre-pandemic or a 60% increase in the rate of projected leavers.

- Seventy-eight percent of teachers reported significant job-related stress (associated to hybrid learning, lack of technical support, personal child care, etc), roughly 50% higher than the general working population.
- Teachers in 2021 reported depression at a rate 2 ½ times greater than the general population.
- Among the many additional stressors reported by teachers during the pandemic, lack of administrator support was reported as a major factor in creating difficult working conditions and resulted in increased stress, depression, and burn out.

In this account, "Teachers' reported probability of leaving their current state or the profession within the next five years (also) increased from 24% on average in March of 2020 to 30% in March 2021. This change was due to a reduction in the percentage of teachers reporting a zero probability of leaving and a corresponding increase in the percentage reporting chances above 50%." Source: *Zamarro, G., Camp, A., Fuchsman, D., & McGee, J. B. (2021). Understanding how COVID-19 has Changed Teachers' Chances of Remaining in the Classroom. Education Reform Faculty and Graduate Students Publications.*

It has been said that employees don't leave organizations, they leave their situation. In the case of educational personnel, this migration is even more impactful as it affects the daily operation of schools in general – and the specific human connections with students and families in particular. In this example, school leaders are charged with creating families in their schools to develop a culture in which school personnel thrive on a personal level as well as professionally.

Schools are different from most other organizations in that the essence of the work done by all members of the faculty and staff contains an enormous human component. We are not interacting with gear motors on an assembly line. Our "products" think, feel, and interact with us. In addition, while we are often doing much of the work as adults in a somewhat solitary location (think a classroom or an office), much of the process also requires us to work collaboratively with others. Sometimes, those other people do the same work as we do, and sometimes, they do work that is quite different but supports our efforts directly. This level of human interaction and symbiosis is helpful in creating families within the school.

SCHOOLS NEED TO CREATE FAMILIES

While you will see that I indeed mean the word literally in some cases, families can also occur when the parties are not related in the traditional sense. I want to be clear that the basic understanding is that family has both positive and negative connotations (I'm talking about you, Uncle Edward). In this section, the concept of family is intended to convey the idea of people who are connected through an identity - working at the school - and spend time together in professional and personal spaces.

I think we would all agree that when considering the work-life balance and enculturation of the adults in our school, one of our highest priorities would be to create an organization where people don't just come to work, but one in which they WANT to come to work. As a principal, I envisioned leading an organization where people get up in the morning and eagerly get ready to come to our school. If you are lucky enough to get to choose most of your staff, you get to create groups of people with complementary talents and strengths. Sometimes, though, you get what you get. The ideas presented in this chapter are pertinent to both situations. Note that in either situation, the family environment does not just happen. Leaders and teachers must continually strive to keep the family functional and productive.

In the world of education, as in most other professions, this balance is rarely achieved. Our reality is that we spend a great portion of our waking lives in the company of our co-workers. It makes sense for those of us who are school leaders to make this time positive in nature and of value to the employee so they are more easily inclined to find satisfaction and stay with the organization for many years. Creating work families helps us increase the likelihood that our staff will want to stay with us.

How Do You Create Families?

Creating a family culture in the educational workplace can be a daunting task. There is nothing easy about putting together people of different ages, backgrounds, and life experiences and forming a cohesive whole. However, it can be done. Here are some things you can do or begin to do right away.

Hire people you know will succeed. If we only had a clean slate and a crystal ball this step would be easy. Hiring to create families is one of the most important things you can do to create successful and long-lasting employees.

Screening applicants online or on paper can be a daunting task and only gives you a limited perspective on how a prospective team member will fit into the community you are trying to create. Put more emphasis on screening applicants for fit, rather than just format. As you consider new hires, a brief survey of your staff can help you know what they feel is needed to complete their family. A few open-ended questions such as, "What does your group do well," or "The one thing our group needs to become better is…" Someone with a background or interest in athletics might fit in well with a group that is interested in providing an after-school running club. Someone who worked in mental health might fit in with a group that is implementing an SEL program or developing a new discipline system. Many school districts use pre-screening tools such as Gallup and AppliTrack to assess potential fit in future employees as part of the application process. Using these assessment tools as part of your screening process can help you look for strengths relative to the team you are building and choose the right people to hire.

Consider hiring from within the community. One of the most successful practices, in my experience, and one that has created a stable school staff with minimal turnover is the practice of hiring from within the community. At one point, I had three sets of sisters that were teachers and a set of brothers that were paraprofessionals working in different areas of our school. I also had several employees that were parents of students working in various places. There is a built-in connection and relationship with the school community for all of these staff members. In the case of the siblings, a positive experience at our school led them to recruit a family member to join our team. Working together they shared and supported each other with the additional benefit of knowing and creating the positive family culture we strove to produce. If you actively recruit family members to your school, you increase the likelihood that they will feel connected and will stay with you. Another valuable outcome of hiring community members is that they can spread correct and, hopefully, positive information about the school to their friends and neighbors. The potential goodwill generated for the school could prove invaluable if issues were to occur at some point. Advertise job openings to your PTO or community social media groups. Ask the parents of your students if they, or someone they know, might be interested in working at the school.

Create groups of people who connect and complement each other. Just like a coach, a school leader is charged with putting together a winning lineup of people who can work collaboratively to create a successful team. Planning your school lineup is a crucial step in this process. When considering groups of people to work together, leaders need to consider the strengths and talents of each member of the team, along with their ability to connect and collaborate with the other members of the team. Putting a highly ambitious or overzealous member on a functioning team does not lead to the longevity of the team even if the outlier is amazingly talented in some area. It is important to note that we are not only looking for staff members to complete our families, but potential staff members are also looking at us as they consider whether to join our community. Our work goes beyond simple selection. We are also required to attract applicants who choose us over other work options.

As an elementary school principal, I created grade-level groups of teachers for our school. One year, I found myself with a set of teachers that did not exactly fit into any of the groups I had thoughtfully created. I decided that these teachers would be placed on a team together with the knowledge that they were particularly suited to working independently, while also being able to maintain the school vision and strive for student success. This worked out perfectly! The teachers in that group, while cordial and able to communicate, did not feel the need to be together all the time. When each of the members of this grade level was part of a different team, they felt like outcasts and did not collaborate well with their group. As "independent contractors" they found their niche. For several years, except for one member who retired, they functioned well together (but apart)! This is one example, but you may also find other contrasts such as pedagogical theories that differ, political leanings of the team members, or cultural factors that create communication issues within the team. Assisting groups to find their commonalities among these differences help with communication and functionality so that these groups can work together effectively.

Honor or create rituals. One solid element of a family work atmosphere is the idea of rituals. Rituals are built into the culture of an organization and serve the function of helping members identify as part of the group. An example of a ritual that binds people to an organization's identity is the annual Indianapolis 500 winner drinking milk from the winner's cup. There are probably more people that know this happens than know why it happens. The why in this case is irrelevant. When you win the Indy 500, you drink milk. Whenever you go on stage to perform, someone is bound to tell you to break a leg. Police officers always touch the rear fender of a car before they approach the driver. Rituals abound in all professions. In schools, we have different rituals that identify us and help our staff become part of our family. Whether the rituals are annual events, special dress days, or something else, they are a big part of branding your organization as a distinct place to be. If you are new to a campus, don't get rid of all the rituals before you know their impact on the school community. One of the best pieces of advice when it comes to changing things up is to make haste, slowly. Think about the rituals that are in place in your organization and find ways to celebrate them.

A PERSPECTIVE FROM THE FIELD

Brian Redmond, High School Band Director, Wyoming

The word family is a very loaded term for many of us, and one that has been, unfortunately at times, used to guilt a little extra work out of employees. Set that aside for a moment, though, and consider your own family (biological or the family you might have found along the way). Family is messy. Family isn't always the rosy picture of the full group sitting around the table at Thanksgiving.

I remember advice I was given when my oldest child was entering the dreaded middle school "tween" years - "There will be many times that you won't like them, but be sure to always love them." For me, you can't have family without love (even when dealing with middle school attitudes and drama).

As I think about a school culture and climate, the longer I teach, the more I think of that advice. I may not always like my coworkers. I know that I will definitely not always like my principals, even the best ones (after all, it can be difficult to always like the person who tells me that I need to cover a class during my planning period, or that I need to come into school after hours to supervise a school event). I can, however, be sure to always love my coworkers... and my principals too.

Now, let me be clear - I am not talking about romantic love. The ancient Greek philosophers described many different kinds of love that a person can experience and share. I am not advocating that anyone go out and make a pass at their coworkers or boss. I doubt your HR director will accept that you did it because a book told you to.

Think about love, for a moment. I love my children. This means making sure that their needs are taken care of. It also means having some tough talks with them - dealing with conflict, disappointment, worry - and helping them meet new challenges in a way that they have a chance to find success. As a teacher, those are all the things that I am delighted to find in an administrator or coworker.

Not every teacher is immediately there. Like the students in their classrooms and the school, some have baggage of past disappointments and frustrations that have taught them to keep their guard up. If your goal is to welcome these teachers into your family, I would encourage you to continue to show them that you are someone they can count on, someone who will follow through, and someone who can make the difficult decisions fairly. When it comes time to make some possibly unpopular decisions, help them know why the decisions are being made and understand how they are impacted.

A STEP-BY-STEP APPROACH TO CREATING FAMILIES
STEP 1 – Hiring is Key

There is probably nothing more impactful to keeping good teachers in your school than hiring good teachers in the first place. This sounds obvious, but there are pitfalls to this idea that can derail your efforts to keep good people in your school. Having a big-picture view of your school is essential to your hiring strategy. We often screen applicants based on information we can see on paper. Certification and employability are important first steps, but it is vital to take into account the needs of a particular department or grade level. When we begin with the idea of creating families we screen with this second lens. In this second screening, look for commonalities that connect to your school. Did the candidate grow up nearby? Did they graduate from a program that connects to other staff members? Do they mention interests that connect with extracurricular clubs that would benefit the group?

STEP 2 – Creating Effective Teams Requires a Coaching Mindset

The winningest coach in NBA history is Gregg Popovich of the San Antonio Spurs. One of the hallmarks of Coach Pop, as he is affectionately called, is his ability to put players together that can function as a team above their ability to function as individual stars. He is also known for drafting players that stay in the organization for many years and identify as Spurs Family. When looking at creating families at school, we can take several lessons from Coach Popovich. First, it's important to look at how the family functions and what is needed to enhance their effectiveness. Second, while there are clearly stars who have immense talent, they are often effective only as individuals and are not necessarily good for the team. In one of my administrative roles, I had a teacher who was a superstar in her own right. Her students were successful, and she put forth great effort to make her class the best. However, her unwillingness or inability to work with her teammates created negativity and division in the group, which spread out to the school as a whole. The group did not benefit from her expertise, and conversely, they suffered from her inability to share techniques and practices with them. People who worked in her group often left the school or asked to be moved to a different team. This created a situation where we were often having to train and develop new people without the benefit of them becoming long-term leaders themselves.

STEP 3 – Provide Opportunities for the Family to be a Family

I am a big believer in creating school and team identity. Teacher families at my school identified with each other as a unit, as well as understood their part in making the whole organization run successfully. Being in an elementary school, my groups were grade levels, and my grade levels were notorious for designing and creating shirts that identified themselves as part of their group. One great example is my fifth-grade teachers who designed a shirt modeled after the famous record album cover of The Beatles' Abbey Road. The shirt consisted of the words Fab Fifth, along with silhouetted images of the five teachers walking across the iconic crosswalk. The encouragement of family identity connects those employees to the smaller unit of their grade level, which on a daily basis is the strongest connection they have to our school as a whole. Encourage your teams to express their family connection whenever possible, and you will create stronger teams that want to stay together.

STEP 4 – Balance Family With Professionalism

There is a school of thought that says that home is home and work is work. This is true, but the idea of creating a school where people feel connected takes into account the fact that people are at the school for the majority of their productive waking hours. When we say that creating a family atmosphere is important, that does not mean literally. Some of the main elements that are part of most families include a power hierarchy based on position and age, among other factors. This is only partially a function of the school family idea. When I was a brand new principal, I was 31 years old, and a majority of the staff were older than me. That situation did not exactly fit the family model as I would have probably been considered the younger brother or son based on the ages of my teachers and staff. It is important when considering how school staff function in a family mode that we maintain professionalism and not create power imbalances based on perceived family roles.

STEP 5 – Make Haste Slowly

This step probably belongs in every chapter, as part of every idea in this book. I cannot stress enough how important it is to move forward at a reasonable pace when making changes in practices and especially in changing culture. No matter what you've been told as a new hire or what you perceive as a veteran, charging ahead full-on without hesitation will almost assuredly scuttle any successful implementation. Just as "Rome was not built in a day," school culture and practices do not change overnight. I am not suggesting that you don't move forward with changes but am simply suggesting that you move ahead in a deliberate manner.

Many years ago, I was interviewed for a principal position in a small city about 200 miles from where my family and I were living. There was clearly a need for change in the culture to the point that I could sense it as I walked into the front door of the school. One of the questions in the interview was, "What would you change in the first 90 days as principal of this school?" My answer was, "Nothing." I knew from the look on the Assistant Superintendent's face that this was the answer he was hoping I'd give. I told them it would take me that long to begin assessing the strengths and weaknesses of the campus and that I would not want to change any of the culture and traditions that were valuable and important to the people in that short time period. Change happens exactly when it happens, and laying the groundwork for accepting change is the first step to having the changes occur. Spend time initially doing this, and your culture-building efforts will assuredly be more successful.

WHAT COULD POSSIBLY GO WRONG?
You are assigned staff you didn't select.
There were times I would have described my schools as homes for wayward teachers. I can cite numerous examples when I had a teacher vacancy and was already screening and interviewing, then was told that I had to take a teacher from another campus. When you don't get to select the staff member, you lose an opportunity to build a family-like team. In this situation, we have the additional task and opportunity to find out more about the new teammate and learn about the value they can bring to the team. My philosophy of accepting staff members who are transferred to my school is two-pronged depending on the reason for the transfer. If the transfer is due to performance issues in another place, I consider the fact that they are being given the gift of being able to start fresh in a new spot. They are focused on being successful, and I am focused on making sure they are successful. If the transfer is due to low enrollment at their previous school I consider the fact that I trust my colleagues to have properly vetted the staff member, and they are going to be great. I can tell you that this proved to be true in almost every case over the years. Do we sometimes get other people's problems? Yes. But we have the influence to mitigate those problems and enculturate these staff members into our great organizations!

Families are sometimes dysfunctional.
There is a real concern that putting people together that are related can cause rifts. When co-workers are a group of

unrelated people, there is a social distance present that can often be of benefit. Personal feelings are rarely part of the equation when discussing work issues. There is a greater focus on the work when it is unencumbered by also navigating the personal relationships present in a family. There are potentially real issues that come into play when considering that "she always acts as if my ideas are less valid." When considering a team of people that have both personal and professional connections, you have to explicitly consider the dynamics of the group, and plan for the potential pitfalls. Roles and responsibilities need to be communicated directly. The personal strengths and weaknesses of the individual members need to be addressed in the function of the group. Not everyone will be expected to be an equal contributor to every project. If one member is better at organizational planning, they should be doing the organizational planning. If another member is better at big picture thinking over details, they should be allowed to do that with the understanding that family dynamics are present but not directive in the group.

Working with community members exposes the organization.

In my experience with hiring parents and community members to work at the school, this potential pitfall is something that definitely needs to be considered. While schools don't typically have a mission to work covertly, it's most often the case that our families do not usually see the everyday inner workings of the school. Usually, this is because most parents drop their children at the door and pick them back up at the door when the school day ends. Having a parent or community member working at the school allows the school structure and idiosyncrasies to be revealed. When the secretary is also a parent and lives in the community, she will have neighbors asking about specific people, activities, and inner working details. It is important when hiring members of the community to discuss the appropriateness of what can be shared. Here's an example: A staff member who comes from the community brings students to the office, or sees students brought in for a disciplinary issue. As an employee they must understand that it would be inappropriate to share the information with other parents due to privacy concerns. They are often placed in a difficult situation where friends and neighbors might ask them for information they cannot provide. This potential situation needs to be addressed at the onset of their employment so they consider their separate roles as parents, community members, and school employees.

I'm only here for the paycheck.
As a leader who loves people and cares about the physical and emotional culture of my workplace, this is a tough one for me. When talking about my work family, I didn't use the term family as a throwaway. We shared each other's lives in a very personal way while working together to create a school environment that modeled personal connection as a means to improving ourselves as learners and community members. All the births, marriages, deaths, illnesses, and triumphs were shared and commemorated. So, when a faculty or staff member chose not to be part of that culture, it could be disconcerting.

While the goal is always 100% of people connecting to the culture, the reality is that some people do not want to be connected to their colleagues for various reasons. I am not talking about people who actively work against the culture, but those who do not want to actively join in. A great example from my practice is a teacher I worked with who was outwardly cool and stand-offish and was part of a team that was completely connected to the point that they vacationed together in the summers. This staff member contributed to grade-level planning and did what needed to be done for the group, but she did not want to talk about her outside life much, or even eat lunch with the other teachers. It was not because she was unfriendly. She just enjoyed solitude at lunchtime and was genuinely uninterested in talking about spouses, kids, trips, or maladies. There were some bad feelings about this among the rest of the group, but the ultimate lesson was that this teacher was there to work and did not find sustenance in being part of the family. In this situation the teachers communicated with each other, learned that there was nothing personal in this behavior, and they were able to continue to function effectively as a group.

A PERSPECTIVE FROM THE FIELD

LaKeyseah Brennan, Virtual Education Specialist, South Carolina

A phrase I always say: "Students will always be students. It is the staff [culture] of the school that makes the difference."

My first year teaching was a wonderful experience.

I had a mentor that texted me before school started and asked if there was anything I needed or ways that she could help me to prepare for the school year. We not only were able to work next door to each other, but we also worked on the same team where we collaborated often. She would host department events where everyone in our department would meet at her house for dinner and games. She would make desserts and cute candy bags for the holidays that were always a small gesture of appreciation.

My hallway would gather in the teacher's lounge every other Friday to bring themed dishes and come together and fellowship. My school would have potlucks during special holidays and encouraged teachers to attend community events which gave us time to see each other outside of school.

Having this culture of a family made my days at school more bearable when things got tough. I created relationships with a few teachers that were a safe space for me and were a sounding board when I was frustrated. This sense of community (100+ staff and 1400 students) was a wonderful experience, and I have always measured my other experiences by this. After six years of teaching at this school, I only left because I did not feel supported by my principal.

Little did I know that the next three years of my teaching career would be the opposite. I spent more time with the new teachers that came in with me and the Assistant Principal Intern, rather than my department or hallway. I felt like I had to seek information on day-to-day operations because no one showed me or told me. I barely saw my department chair even though she was down the hall from me. I would sit in meetings with teachers who taught the same content as me, and they were asking me for ideas and help. I felt like the teachers were draining. They always complained, never wanted to collaborate, and it always felt like a competition between them and me. The first week I was there, a teacher friend who switched to the same school as me and I decided that we would implement a new teacher committee or different events to create a positive school culture among the staff. By my third year, our hall celebrated birthdays every month, collected monetary donations, a card, and a lunch time potluck for everyone in the hall; sometimes, we would extend an invitation to the administrative staff or other teachers. We had such a great time coming together and being intentional about building a positive culture that the teachers upstairs and the front office staff started to do the same thing in their own way.

Ironically, when I left both of those schools, the celebrations and intentional moments to build relationships ended.

I am not saying that all schools are able to do these same things because it does take work, but it definitely set the tone for different moments in my teaching career.

Although I am at my third school, I feel like my love for teaching has been revived. I have a few relationships I have built that continue to push me to grow as a teacher. I have one teacher who is friendly, likes to host events, encourages me to try new tech lessons for student engagement, and then on the other hand I have a new teacher who likes to hold planning parties in our classroom after school with snacks and order a pizza. These relationships help sustain my love for teaching. And when there are days that every lesson fails, I can go to them and they always offer kind words and no judgment.

I attended a coaching teacher (interns/new teachers) meeting, and they spoke on ways coaching could be used to help with teacher retention once interns complete their education program. I heard a lot of educators say things about how they have worked with interns who would have a great experience in their program at the university, a great experience during their practicum, then hate their first to fifth year teaching and leave the profession. They wanted to blame this on the new teachers/interns not receiving the proper coaching. I raised my hand and shared that interns/new teachers could have had a great experience with their education program and their practicum experience, but if the school where they are hired does not have a positive school culture it will drive them away from the profession.

In my ten years of teaching, I have experienced a school that nurtured my love for teaching, almost shattered my love for teaching, and one that currently reignites my love for teaching each day.

When I think about a family at work, it looks like teamwork (team focused), collaboration (willingness to share thoughts and ideas, trust in ability and with concerns), growth (push each other to be successful), frequent communication, and it all has to be done together with intentionality.

HOW BUILDING FAMILIES WORKED IN PRACTICE

Several years ago, I had the opportunity to create a bilingual education program at my school where one had not previously existed. I had to hire all the bilingual teachers in one summer, one for each grade level in my school. I was able to place a currently employed teacher in one of the positions as she was already certified, willing, and able to teach a bilingual class. The other teachers I had to find. One of the new hires was a transfer I knew from another school and who knew the teacher that was at my school already. They were excited to be working together, and I was confident they would bond and create a successful team. If you have ever attempted to hire specially certified staff you know this is not an easy task. There are often very few applicants for the positions.

I was fortunate enough to interview and hire a newly graduated and certified teacher from a local university who I sensed was going to become an educational superstar. After she was officially hired, she came to visit me and asked if I was still looking for teachers to fill the bilingual roster. I was and was not having great luck with many of the candidates I was screening and interviewing. This newly hired teacher told me about two of her newly graduated classmates that she worked closely with at the university and asked if I was interested in considering them for positions. They had not applied in our district, and I told her I would love to meet them. So, she contacted her two friends. Within a day, they had both applied in our district, I interviewed them and hired them both. These three teachers were already connected, and because the two were hired based on the recommendation of the third member of their group, they were more inclined to work hard and be successful.

These three teachers came to me as a set; essentially an already-created family. They were happy to come to work every day in a new environment and a new program with ready-made colleagues and trusted friends. They pushed each other to do better and held each other accountable for doing a great job as teachers. The best part of having created this family environment for them was that as each of them was also on different grade levels, there were additional benefits that came from the connection. One of those benefits was that they were able to create a vertical alignment of curriculum that does not come easily in an elementary school. Another benefit was that as they were also members of their grade level teams (separate from each other), they brought together different groups of teachers that did not always spend time together.

These teachers were hired over a dozen years ago as of this writing. One of the teachers is still at that school creating magic for bilingual students in her classroom. The other two have since moved into administrative roles as elementary school principals. The bilingual program at that school started strong because much thought had been put into creating a family of teachers.

A PERSPECTIVE FROM THE FIELD

Dr. Pedro J. Cabrera, MJE, Professor of Communication and Journalism, Texas

There's something special about coming back from summer break, walking into the building, realizing the A/C had JUST been turned up, walking to my room, opening my door, noticing everything is all over the place because the custodians waxed the floor, seeing my neighbor walk by, heading over and talking for 15 minutes about our summer adventures, all before that first professional development, all before even touching anything to prepare. At that moment, I wasn't concerned about prepping for the upcoming school year because I knew I may never have substantial time to do so. I was wanting to immediately catch up with my classroom neighbor - as if I hadn't seen them in forever, but really, it was just a couple of weeks.

We all have that feeling - seeing each other, giving hugs, telling them "welcome back." Then, the teacher down the hall walked in with their bags, and a 15-minute conversation turned into 30, then 45, then an hour, all before the first faculty meeting in the morning.

Welcome Back.

I didn't do anything. I didn't touch my desk. I didn't touch any desk - I caught up with other teachers who - when the first day of school came, would be in the trenches with me as we rowed forward. That is what building a positive school culture is all about - building those relationships with each other outside those regular school-related topics.

Welcome Back.

That is the same thing teachers need to do with their students. They won't work for teachers they don't like. They don't owe you respect - more times than not, you are a new stranger to them. We must earn our students' respect. We must create an environment in which they want to be in your classroom so the learning and classroom management process goes well for the teacher. That means spending substantial time at the beginning of the school year to get to know your students. That sounds like the first line in a Teaching 101 manual, but it needs to be reinforced that creating a culture in which students - and teachers - want to be in the building is what will lead to success.

It starts with welcoming everyone back. Welcome teachers back to their home away from home, a place that should feel like we're all in this together. Welcome students back into our classrooms, a place they know they will learn and feel safe, that the person at the front of the room is not only going to teach them, but they're going to have a good day every day in that room.

Welcome Back.

A FINAL THOUGHT ABOUT CREATING FAMILIES IN SCHOOLS

So often we hear an expression such as, "We are all one big family here at Bestever Elementary."While this sometimes strikes us as more words than deeds, it does get to the heart of the desire to create a school culture that contains the positive elements of the family feel. Connections before content is an expression that not only applies to the teacher-student relationship but also to the administrator-faculty and faculty-faculty relationship as well.

If one of the main reasons people leave organizations is that they don't feel connected, it's important for those of us who are leaders to help create a culture where people find connections. Sometimes, it's with the other people, and often, it's with the community in general. Whenever we as leaders can pull in the loose threads of our staff and find places where they connect, we are on the way to having our people hang around for a long time.

CHAPTER 2
Teachers Need Real, Appropriate Autonomy
Leaders Need to Let Decision-Making Happen at the Correct Level

"Autonomy is different from independence. It means acting with choice."
~Daniel H. Pink

WHEN TEACHERS HAVE TRUE AUTONOMY THEY FEEL CONNECTED TO THE ORGANIZATION

I want to call this story "A Tale of Two Days." When I was a first-year teacher in Houston, Texas back in 1983, I had an incredible class of 31 first graders who were bright, inquisitive, challenging, and connected. I remember planning (by myself) my entire first day of school lessons and activities. I did as I had been taught – I included read-aloud time, writing time, reading lessons, math activities, social studies activities, and a science lesson. I was ready to go! I got down to the lessons and was doing what I thought was a great job considering it was my first day teaching ever. My class had lunch at 10:30 AM that year and when we got to lunchtime, I realized that I had completed every bit of the lesson plan I had written. There was going to be an issue when we got back from lunch, and I was not sure how I would finish out the day. I ended up asking the seasoned teacher next door what she had planned for the day, and she shared a bunch of lessons on creating routines and procedures, handwriting, and classroom games for centers. I was winging it, but I got through that first day with those students and re-planned the rest of the first week by adding many new activities and procedures, and it went pretty well!

I had been given independence at that point, but what I really needed was autonomy. The second part of this story happened about eight weeks later. I was starting to really click with my class, and we were spending some very productive days learning to read and write among other things. In those days in Houston, teachers did not have duty-free lunch periods, so I took my class to lunch one day as usual and spent the time in the cafeteria monitoring them. As we re-entered the classroom, I flipped on the lights and was surprised to see two district office people in my classroom with clipboards and concerned looks on their faces. As my students filed back into the room, one of them told me, "Mr. Silverman, there are several things wrong with your classroom. Let's start here and work our way around." She motioned to my chalkboard and began with the size I had written my letters, continued with the structure of my student journals, the height of my bookcase, and a few other things I honestly don't remember. For a moment I was taken aback, and then I was secretly amused. None of the things she mentioned were serious (to me). They were all stylistic and focused on the visual expectations of the district. (I kid you not, I was handed a thick book called the Houston ISD Style Manual.)

At this point, I felt like I was given neither independence NOR autonomy. It occurred to me that decisions for my students should be made closest to them, which was by me in my classroom. The Style Manual was obtrusive and invasive, It seemed to put more emphasis on how the journals looked rather than what was inside them. It made me question rules and procedures that were initiated far away from the kids (my expression for this is "decisions made by people who work on carpet for people who work on tile") and helped me understand that teacher autonomy was vital to making sure decisions that were best for our students were made in the correct place.

TEACHERS NEED REAL, APPROPRIATE AUTONOMY

It is important to first understand the definition of *autonomy* and *independence* as we discuss this topic. Autonomy is self-direction. People who work autonomously do not work alone in a vacuum. The drive to act comes from inside the person. Independence is not being influenced by outside forces. Independent workers don't connect to the organizational goals or their colleagues, instead, they work to their own ends. If the goal is to promote teacher autonomy we have tons of opportunities to provide meaningful ways for teachers to be self-directed. If you read survey results from teachers or look at educational social media, you'll find that one thing that drives away our best teachers is the feeling that they are micromanaged.

Our goal as leaders should be to ensure that we trust our people to do what's right for our students and families. If we continue to only engage from the place where we are telling people what to do in all aspects of their job, we will create a situation where people "buy out" rather than "buy in." We risk losing our teachers imperceptibly at first. We tell them what to do in lieu of them using their decision-making and creativity. They begin disconnecting from the organization because they are not invested. The weakened connections help them make the decision to leave when a different opportunity arises.

How do you Create a Culture of Real Autonomy for Teachers?

The answer to this question is either easy or difficult depending on your leadership style. When it comes to thinking about teacher autonomy you have to consider your own ideas about issues such as control and trust. You will always hear that as a school leader the "buck stops with you" and that you bear the ultimate responsibility for everything that happens in your organization. This is essentially true, and you will find leaders who interpret this as meaning that they need to have their hand in everything. At its extreme, this plays out with leaders micromanaging every facet of what happens in their organization. The flip side of this (theoretically) is the leader who says I trust my people to do what is right and only need to know the highlights of what is going on here. Members of this organization are independent and often make decisions that are best for themselves in all areas with little to no consideration about how the decision affects the students or the school.

The sweet spot for creating a culture of autonomy is to find the balance between hands way on and hands way off. Think of the analogy of the group rowing the boat. In a micromanaged culture, the captain not only tells everyone exactly how to row but often takes over the rowing completely themselves. The boat does not benefit from the strength and talent of the rowers in the group. In the independent culture, everyone rows the way they like without concern about moving the boat in any particular direction. The captain stays out of the way and does not provide any structure or direction. The boat goes in circles or veers way off course.

How do you create a culture of autonomy?
Communicate the goals of the organization: If you don't know where you are going, how do you know when you get there? One of the biggest pitfalls in leadership is believing that everyone knows the targets. You would think in a

school there would be obvious goals. All students should achieve academically at a high level. Students and staff should feel safe, loved, and honored in the school community. Parents should be involved partners in their child's education. And while these are typically what we want from schools none of these are really measurable. The way to reach these goals can be radically different based on the ideology, talent, and experience of the staff members. It is the duty of the school leader to not only provide these vague overarching goals but to be specific about how each will look and feel when they are achieved.

We have to identify a starting and ending point to determine if we are meeting our goals. Staff members want to work in an organization that is going somewhere specific. Once the goals are obviously met we can all celebrate our success and set our next goals. What is obvious to us may not be obvious to someone else, so it is important to make sure we all understand where we are headed.

Build capacity by letting go: Just as we should strive to do with our students, the way to build strength, capacity, and pride in our staff is to communicate goals, provide structure and support, and then let them go! People want to work where they believe their contributions matter, not where they are treated as a non-essential cog that can be replaced by anyone else at a moment's notice. If our goal is to build and retain teachers that choose to stay with our organization it is of vital importance that we develop not only their capacity as teachers but their specific value as their essential selves. The unspoken message of the micromanager is, "I need you here to monitor these students, but anyone can do this because I am making all the decisions." By allowing teachers the autonomy to interpret the methods they use to reach the goals, we value their unique contributions to our school community. Help communicate the goals, and then get out of the way.

This is probably the most difficult piece for leaders who worry about their ultimate responsibility for the organization, but it is the most important to accept. The enormity of managing all the moving parts of a school dictates that we cannot possibly be everywhere or be everything to everybody. If we attempt to lead every meeting, plan every unit, and attend every event, we are creating an untenable situation that will cause us to burn out quickly and be of little use to the organization.

Most importantly, one of our most significant goals as school leaders is to build and grow our people. When we dictate, plan, and script we inadvertently send the message that we don't believe our people are capable of doing these things on their own. The message needs to be that we trust them to be effective based on what they know and their understanding of our shared goals.

Determine what can be self-selected and what can not: Some things we do are not negotiable. We may have requirements from our state and local authorities that must be implemented such as what skills are taught in a specific content area in a specific grade. We may be experts on the political situation in Nepal but are teaching 3rd grade. Creating autonomous practices involves knowing what is flexible and what is not. There may be a specific set of skills taught, but is the calendar of when they're taught flexible? That could be an area where teachers are given the autonomy to map out the order they teach concepts. If there is a Language Arts concept, can they choose the book they use to teach it?

Autonomy allows our teachers to make critical decisions on how they teach concepts as opposed to what concepts to teach. It is important to make that distinction and allow for different ways to reach the agreed-upon goals for the year. This also extends to the use of specific classroom materials, technology, textbooks, etc. If we are able to allow teachers to select the materials and media they use to teach concepts, we honor their expertise and experience. If something is not mandated, it's negotiable!

Truly collaborate on annual appraisals: When we work with teachers on their annual appraisal package we often use a prescribed system of goal-setting, observation, feedback, conferencing, and evaluation of progress. Allowing teachers the autonomy to set specific goals is a crucial part of creating a culture of autonomy. While we cannot often scrap the entire prescribed system, we can always make the continuous improvement cycle personal for different teachers.

On one hand, you may have a brand-new teacher right out of school. They may not have the experience to know how to set goals for student performance and the steps needed to get there. In this case, you will have to be more prescriptive as you teach them the process. However, you may also have a teacher with years of experience and a strong sense of where they are going and how to get there. In this case, you can allow them to take the lead in setting goals and focus on the end product without interfering with the details of how they gets there. Through collaboration, you find that the appraisal system works differently for different people.

Furthermore, while the cycle may be the same for all, there will be vast differences in how the goals will look for a special education Life Skills teacher, a Welding teacher, and a fifth-grade teacher. Collaborating and listening to the teacher throughout the cycle will allow them the autonomy to take a leadership role in setting goals reasonable to their situation, and will allow you to take on a more collegial role in the process.

A PERSPECTIVE FROM THE FIELD

Andrew Holmes, Math Curriculum Specialist, Texas

In education, especially now, it is important to take into consideration a variety of factors when determining how to support/grow a teacher. Currently, we are experiencing a significant shortage of teachers, and many new teachers are alternatively certified. I myself had to pursue the alternative certification route. Education was not my first, second, or even third choice of careers. My background before education included managing a large retail store with over 200 employees on payroll. I had several employees that were teachers, and I always thought they had it easy. My educational career began when I made the decision to quit my job cold turkey and move to a larger city. After not finding work I became a long-term substitute in a life skills classroom. The principal at the school saw something in me, and I spent five amazing years learning my craft. Eventually, my wife and I moved to a new city, and I had to change schools. I had the worst experience of my teaching career. One of the frustrating procedures the school had was how feedback was given. At the time, two glows and a grow was a popular strategy for providing observational feedback. Basically, the administrator would identify two things you did well and one thing they wondered about or thought you could do better. After each walkthrough you reflect and try to do better the next time. The problem became that teachers adapted the mentality "I am never going to be good enough." Eventually, you find yourself not being concerned about the feedback because it doesn't feel genuine. Also, there was no reinforcement or praise for addressing the feedback and doing better. This was one factor in the faculty, including myself, having a low morale. Looking back, I think the strategy was good, but I don't think every observation from an administrator needs to include constructive criticism. It is important to me that the administrator not approach constructive feedback with a one size fits all approach.

A STEP-BY-STEP APPROACH TO CREATING A CULTURE OF TEACHER AUTONOMY

STEP 1 – Ensure your organizational goals are clearly understood

When you don't understand where you are and where you are going, it's difficult to give your staff the autonomy to make impactful decisions. What is even worse is if you DO know where you are and where you are going, but you are the only one that knows the goal. In that instance, you can envision the path, but because others don't know the goals they will often simply guess, take action, and appear to be unable to be trusted to do the right thing.

Consider setting your goals collaboratively, and identify the general path to success from all angles. This will create opportunities for staff members to work autonomously. Consider using problem analysis protocols that identify the needs of your organization and involve as many people as practical in the work. There is usually no need for any more than cursory oversight of the daily operations when leadership and the staff are rowing in the same direction. Remember, autonomous does NOT mean independent, and when you do the work to make the goals understandable, you are ensuring that staff members know where to row!

STEP 2 – Fix your mindset

You've read the books, collaborated with colleagues, and have decided that you want to create a more autonomous culture for teachers. However, there is that nagging thing in your head that keeps telling you that you bear the ultimate responsibility for everything that happens in your building.

How do you get from where you are to a different perspective?

Ultimately, you just have to do it. A purposefully obvious change in perspective needs to happen before you can envision an autonomous culture. Examine your level of trust and your tolerance of risk. Truly consider the talents, abilities, and motivation of your staff. If you have relatively stable, mostly experienced staff that are able to work with minimal guidance, it's time to let them run. If you don't then you may need to start very slowly. Your mindset will determine how far you realistically can go right now, but the first thing you need to do is to open your mind to letting go of some control.

STEP 3 – Choose your battles

When you are a leader that hopes and intends for your staff to have true autonomy, you often find yourself tied up in circumstances, not of your own making. Curriculum often has mandated pieces that are not considered to be negotiable. For example, a district may specify which materials are to be used to teach math, which books are to be taught for Freshman English, and which interventions are to be used for students who are in need of assistance. This is an area where teachers feel the least autonomy. As a leader, you want your best teachers to do what they do best. However, there are times when you have to work within a prescriptive situation.

The best advice I can give is to choose your battles. If you cannot allow teachers to choose the materials, you can often allow them to choose the supporting activities that go with the materials. If a certain novel is required, perhaps the teacher can be allowed to choose how a student demonstrates their understanding of the main points. Conversely, if a common assessment is mandated, perhaps you can allow a teacher to choose materials that help students demonstrate the expected mastery of standards.

This is not to suggest that you should never question and, certainly, not support your effective teaching staff. Rather, it requires you to both meet the expectations set for you by whoever makes those choices AND to use your influence to attempt to make change within the system. This is the time to have conversations with the decision-makers and work to get things changed so your effective teachers have the autonomy to use their unique skills to teach their students.

STEP 4 – Make your annual appraisal process inclusionary

Typical annual appraisals are very often one-way activities. The teacher sets goals and we approve them. The teacher performs, and we assess the performance. The teacher reflects on the performance, and we communicate our perception of areas of strength and areas of growth. While there is some voice from the teacher, the ultimate interpretation sits fully with the administrator.

While these may be the required pieces of your district and state evaluation process, there are things you can do to enhance teacher's voice and allow some autonomy in the process. For example, allowing teachers to video a lesson and walk you through the unseen things that are going on can be an enormous help when watching a live lesson later. Knowing more about the students and their dynamics is preferable to a snapshot view where someone might not appear in a flattering light. In addition, rather than only prescribing growth targets for common assessments, a mutual conversation about different ways to show growth can be very helpful in seeing a more rounded picture of how a class is progressing. Giving increased voice to the teacher shows not only that you value their insight and opinion, but it gives them more skin in the game when it comes to their annual appraisal process.

WHAT COULD POSSIBLY GO WRONG?
I understand, but I don't agree.
In every organization, you are going to encounter people who understand the goals of the organization but do not agree with them. They are often part of the process of creating these goals, but when it came to a consensus they agreed to the goals in the group. However, in their mind, they were still not on board. In books, we learn about groups that are transformed and united, but in real life we are sometimes still prisoners of our own mindset. When you have people on the team who know the goals but don't agree, they are not ready to work autonomously.

The best reaction to this is to continue to create a culture where expressing dissent is OK. When dissent is out in the open, you are able to continue discussions and allow other viewpoints to be considered. You certainly do not want to surround yourself with "yes" people. No growth happens in a situation like that. You want to create momentum to improve and hear the voices of those who disagree with the goal of moving the organization forward.

I'm afraid if we allow people to do whatever they want we will fail.
This is the real and often unspoken fear of a leader who is giving up what they consider to be control of all aspects of their organization. It is easy for the naturally collaborative leader to say that this is misguided. However, as part of growing as a leader and creating a culture where teachers want to stay, we are required to give up some of our direct control and allow others to have a say in what happens on a daily basis.

Again, this is a real fear, and you are not wrong to worry about giving up control if you are used to managing/micromanaging in your role. While the leader is usually the one to take the blame for things that don't go right, we are also the ones that receive the praise when things go spectacularly. Part of changing your mindset is making the shift from a deficit thought process to a growth mindset. People who are empowered and given autonomy, when they know the goals of the organization, are much more likely to put forth the effort required to create environments where growth is at the center. This is the environment that stimulates and encourages staff members to continue to grow with us rather than leaving to find a more autonomous situation. It's not only about what can go wrong, it's also about what could go right!

I am hesitant to push back on our Curriculum (or other) Department.
Most people who are drawn to education as a career are pretty awesome, nice people. As a rule, they value collaboration and getting along with others. This often leads us to not question decisions that are made for us that affect

our daily work. If you are like me, you expect the people making decisions to be doing the right thing for the right reason. However, one of my most used expressions when working with other administrators is "Those of us who work on carpet need to remember the effect of our decisions on those who work on tile." What I mean by this is that decisions made outside of the place where people are actually doing the work must take into consideration the actual implementation of our ideas.

We often don't want to push back too strongly on decisions that restrict teacher autonomy. But when we want to create situations where strong teachers are allowed to practice their craft with minimal intrusion, we need to be willing to reject a one-size-fits-all model and push for allowing some on-the-spot decision-making. We are not questioning the content of the decision for some (or even most) of our staff. We are asking for some teachers to be allowed to make curricular decisions based on their proven success. Some teachers love to be told what to teach and how. Others do not. When we intervene to ask for that distinction we are helping create a culture that recognizes individual strengths… the exact culture we stress for our students!

If staff members self-assess they will not see their own flaws (or they will overstate them).
To say it takes all kinds to make a world is truly an understatement. Self-awareness is a tricky business. Some people see themselves as much more effective than they truly are while others are self-deprecating to the point of annoyance. While this can really affect the quality of staff evaluation, we help create a culture of autonomy when we first seek to understand, then solicit feedback from the

people who are being evaluated. Intention and interpretation are key elements in teacher and staff performance, and both of those gain value when the person actually performing the task gives input.

The danger of self-evaluation as a tool is when it is not USED as a tool, but instead is used as the total evaluation. "Just tell me what you want me to put down" is a phrase I've heard used before by harried administrators pushed right up to a deadline to get evaluations completed. There is sometimes relief from the one being evaluated in this case, but people who truly need and want to grow professionally need the external view of their performance and the interpretation from someone outside of themself. So, the potential danger here is that the autonomy has to hit the sweet spot between fully hands-on and fully hands-off. There is a need for true collaboration and perspective that will create conversations where growth and improvement are the key and each person will feel as if they contributed to that growth.

CREATING A CULTURE OF TEACHER AUTONOMY - A REAL-LIFE EXAMPLE

Sometimes, it's difficult to answer a question directly when you are asked. Many years ago, I was working in a school that predominantly served students in poverty. We served a great community, though many of our students were having a difficult time meeting the standards set by the district and state. Early in November one year, I was asked by the Kindergarten team to meet with them to discuss some of the issues they were having with their student progress toward their learning goals. When we gathered they asked, "What are we going to do about these students?!?"

Immediately, my mind went into solutions mode. I had three or four suggestions that were waiting to get from my mind to my mouth, but instead, I said, "What ARE you going to do?" There was some silence, and then a few ideas began to flow from various teachers. Ultimately, they developed a plan to host a family day at school featuring a Thanksgiving feast along with some specific strategies the families could use to support literacy development at home. They set up mock learning stations, small group demonstrations, provided home library books, magnetic letters with metal cookie sheets for home use, and vocabulary development ideas. The event was a success!

After the event when we were considering what had worked in that process, one of the teachers suggested that we plan a spring event as well. Our district educational foundation offered teacher grants up to $5,000 for projects, and they were going to present a proposal. That proposal was funded, and the spring event was even more beneficial for our families and students. The school district became aware of the events and suggested that this group of teachers apply for a state educational grant for $150,000 to expand the program to other grade levels in our school. That grant was ALSO funded, and the teachers who developed this structure were not only elated, but became professionally empowered. They put in a proposal to present at a national conference and were accepted. That group of teachers became connected to each other, our school, our district, our profession, and most importantly, to our families.

It would have been exceedingly easy to have answered that question for those teachers and maybe my ideas would have led to effective practice (or not). But by encouraging autonomy from this group of teachers, they became empowered to help solve their problems, meet our school and district goals, and enhance themselves professionally. Two of the teachers eventually became early childhood specialists, then city- and nation-wide consultants. Their professional growth was directly related to their ability to be autonomous in a critical situation. When I think about how proud I am of them, I'm really glad I held my tongue that November day!

A PERSPECTIVE FROM THE FIELD

Melissa Johnston, Former Colorado and North Carolina High School English Teacher

I have taught high school English for the last 18 years and have loved it for different reasons. The best reason to stay in a position, though, is appropriate teacher autonomy. Teacher autonomy definitely promotes teacher retention, but it can be both a blessing and a curse. How much autonomy does a teacher need or want? How much is too little or too much? I have worked at schools that gave me full autonomy over my curriculum and have worked at schools with scripted curriculums with common assessments and a strict calendar to follow regardless of whether or not students are ready to move on. There has to be a happy medium.

Teachers want the autonomy to teach to the standards how they see fit and with content they are passionate about, but they also want the district to provide resources for them so they can either use them outright (read: brand new teacher) or use them as guidelines to develop something more creative that they know will better suit their students' needs (veteran teacher). It is overwhelming for a teacher to walk into a new position with no resources at all, but it is underwhelming for a teacher to walk into a position where everything is scripted, especially when said teacher hasn't even had a chance to learn the students' wants and needs. I have been in both situations and can honestly say that this is where administrator leaders can really help teachers out.

When administration provides resources that allow us to work autonomously within our classrooms, we are able to develop great plans for students. When admin provides opportunities for us to observe other teachers and other schools to see what they are doing well, we are able to use these observations to further develop our own autonomy to better serve our students.

A great personal example I have from this collaboration leading to autonomy is when I had a superintendent who wanted to implement Project Based Learning (PBL) into our school district. He sent a team of teachers and school leaders to several different schools to see how it was being implemented. After our observations were complete, we were able to debrief and plan together. The observations and planning gave us the resources we needed to give PBL a try while giving us the autonomy to figure out our own PBL units within our own classrooms.

A FINAL THOUGHT ON AUTONOMY

Understanding the difference between independence and autonomy is a key factor in developing a school culture where teachers want to stay because they know their perspectives matter. While it can be scary to give up our perceived control, it should also be our goal to grow and develop our teachers as professionals with a purpose. People who have a say tend to stay. Allowing ourselves to let go and trust our staff is not something you DO, but something you BECOME. It involves the process of picking the right people and having them in the right places, communicating our goals clearly, and trusting (but encouraging and verifying) that all the rowers are moving in the same direction.

CHAPTER 3
Manage Workload by Mastering the Calendar
Avoiding Cool-of-June Thinking
to Create a Balanced Organization

*"Time is really the only capital
that any human has
and the only thing
he can't afford to lose."*
~Albert Einstein

WE CREATE IMBALANCE WHEN WE DON'T CONSIDER DAILY AND YEARLY TIME MANAGEMENT

Staff Olympics seemed like a great idea. I was working late one June afternoon when the typical South Texas heat was blazing outside, but I was in my cool, quiet office. Creating a calendar of events for the upcoming school year was my project for the day, and I was looking at an event that would create excitement and camaraderie for the students and staff in anticipation of the next year's testing season. Absent from the daily school year distractions, I was making incredible progress toward my goal of having the activities calendar finished before I took some time off for a summer break.

I added Staff Olympics to the calendar for the Friday before testing week. I thought that it would create a nice break in the preparation cycle; a time to pause and focus on something other than testing. Staff members would participate in fun events in front of the students and show them that, sometimes, we have to do things that are uncomfortable, but ultimately turn out OK. Staff members would receive medals for winning events, and the kids would cheer them on to victory. It would be so much fun!

Unfortunately, I would find out that some important issues would arise around this event. Several teachers balked at the idea of appearing "foolish" in front of their students and colleagues. A few staff members had medical issues that would preclude them from participating in the sun or in anything that involved running. Some thought the timing was going to be terrible. They were planning to use the Friday before testing to create calm spaces in their classrooms to lower the intensity, rather than ramp it up.

Education is one of the few professions that have an annual beginning and end. We have a set calendar to fill (or not fill) and planning that calendar without intentionally considering the factors that will be in play during that time can create major pitfalls. One of the ways we can create spaces to keep our staff engaged but also maintain balance is by managing our daily and yearly calendars.

MANAGING WORKLOAD BY MASTERING THE CALENDAR

The example I gave above about calendar planning during the summer is one I frequently describe as "Cool-of-June Thinking." When you are sitting in your cool office in June when other staff have already left for their summer break, you are not always able to fully consider how the plans you make will play out when the time really comes. It's easy to plan solo in the Cool of June. However, we do a much better job when we plan based on typical seasonal ebbs and flows. We also improve our planning when we plan outside of a vacuum. Bringing in the voices of others helps us do a much more effective job of planning a calendar that works for the students, staff, and community!

How do you Begin Managing the Calendar?

I read a book once called, *If You Don't Feed the Teachers They Eat the Students*. It's a nifty guide full of tips on how to build community (among other things) in your school. Thinking of this book helps me consider how to effectively plan activities and events for the school. As principal, my role is to create a space where teachers and staff can work to do their best for students all year round. It is also important to consider the people and how the calendar affects their balance.

This chapter is designed to help you look at your overall management of time through the lens of the school calendar. It starts with the most basic assumption. Our staff wants to do what's best for our students and community every day. I truly believe that nobody comes to work at a school intending to create chaos and disharmony. When we endeavor to create sensibility in our calendar we go a long way toward creating a culture that is sustainable all year.

Over my many years in public education, I've noticed there is an ebb and flow to the school year that is almost predictable. These are the items to consider as you plan during those cool June days in the office:

Examine your annual calendar: As I wrote this, I was coming to the close of the current school year. While anticipating the activities that needed to happen before the end of school, I was looking at a packed calendar of summative events. In the few days left with teachers and students, we would have awards ceremonies, a school dance, Field Day, summative appraisal conferences, a presentation to students from a performer, end-of-year special education IEP meetings, lists and letters for students to attend summer school, and a few other odds and ends.

When I was creating the calendar of events for that school year, all of those events had passed. In addition, during the winter it seemed like it would be a great idea to end the year with some significantly fun activities for our students, staff, and community. Once we were in the throes of it all, I could clearly see the effect on staff members (and myself). I had heard the expression, "there's tired, and then there's end-of-the-school-year-teacher tired." It was evident that we were in that stage!

On the Monday after students and teachers left, my intention was to sit down with the calendar for the next school year and make one significant change to the way it was created. I had already asked for a group of people to sit down with me while the tiredness was still fresh in our minds so we could logically and purposefully develop the calendar for the next school year. While there was always a better time for certain events, we intended to mindfully plan the big pieces of the calendar first (testing dates, holidays, district events), then sprinkle in the additional events during the year to make sure we were not overwhelming people.

Consider the daily schedule and the effect on people: There are very few absolutes in elementary education, but one I know is true is that the more students that are on the playground at one time, the more often disciplinary issues arise. At one school I worked at, free play and exploration were encouraged. Free play builds the capacity of students to make decisions and solve problems. However, since school is like a laboratory where kids try things out to see how they work, there were times when that exploration led to poor choices. A result of this that I experienced with staff members was increased frustration. One way to ease this frustration was to consider the daily schedule and maximize the time available for teaching, learning, and exploration.

Playground space was a hot commodity on my campus. Students (and teachers) often want to use the playground at the same time which causes a chaotic mix of too much movement and too many students in the same place at the same time. One way to solve this is to use staff input to create a daily schedule that provides long, uninterrupted teaching blocks that are interspersed with periods of movement. This seems easy, but when you are choreographing that movement among 45 or so different classes it can be difficult.

The solution to this was to sit down with a group of people and block out the daily schedule for different groups that maximized their classroom time and sensibly blocked out time for unstructured activities, lunch periods, specials/electives, and special area services. We used a visual timeline to ensure there wouldn't be hundreds of students all trying to be in the same place at the same time. This helped reduce stress on staff members and maximized the time students spent both in class and enjoying unstructured time in the school day.

Meetings vs Emails: In my educational world, meetings most often occurred after the students were dismissed for the day. Our school day began at 7:30 AM and students were dismissed at 2:55 PM. By the time all students had boarded buses, left the campus walking, or were picked up in cars it was usually 3:20. Our faculty meetings began at 3:30. In Texas, there are not specifically designated contractual hours, but our faculty meetings always began after the generally accepted teacher workday. Most teachers understand there will be duties that require them to work past their hours, but as leaders, we need to be aware that routinely asking people to work past their hours disrespects the boundaries between professional and personal life. Time is a limited commodity, and we need to be aware of how we use it.

My personal practice was to not have a full-on faculty meeting unless the content required us to be together, or the issues required discussion and input. Topics that are purely informational or what I call "administrivia" can be shared in other ways – quick visits to individuals, emails, or texts. When planning the calendar, I asked staff to keep afternoons open and to avoid making appointments and such on Tuesdays if possible. Though we used these Tuesday afternoons on a very sporadic basis for meetings, it was the general consensus that if we needed to meet, it would be on a Tuesday.

The issue of holding meetings vs sending emails can easily become imbalanced, and create school culture issues if we are not careful. There is a benefit to having staff together in one room considering a common issue. As someone who did not hold weekly (sometimes not even monthly) whole staff meetings, I've found that sometimes we had staff members who didn't know each other to the point of not being able to even identify each other by name and face. It's good practice to build a culture where the school community is familiar with each other, and having rare meetings can hinder this. However, meeting just to meet is also not a good idea. Considering the balance of using the time to build culture and share information is important to build a community where staff feels like their time is valued.

Create duty schedules that work for staff: Teachers and staff are very often called upon to perform duties outside the classroom. Arrival duty, bus duty, lunch duty, playground duty, dismissal duty, and more are part of the operation of a school. When assigning duties school leaders often create the schedules in a vacuum. Names are put into spots, and off we go. A better solution might be to create a duty sign-up system where people can choose duties that work not only for the school but for their lives.

For example, I had staff members who ran their own children to different schools in the mornings. Morning duty was difficult for them and created an issue when they were trying to be in two places at one time. I have often been told that this is one of the reasons teachers leave the school and take another position closer to home or in the same district as their children attend. If these staff members, who want to stay and contribute to our school community, could perform other duties that fit their schedule better, we can create a situation where they are more likely to stay.

If we can consider these issues and allow staff to choose their duties based on their schedules and preferences, we can not only get everything covered, but we can retain these valuable staff members.

A STEP-BY-STEP APPROACH TO PLANNING OUT THE YEAR TO SUPPORT YOUR STAFF (AND YOURSELF!)

STEP 1 – August is a time of hope and possibility. Staff members are coming off summer vacation, and they are excited for the new school year. Their minds are on getting their rooms prepared, their lessons planned, and the summer ideas or PD learning more focused for their new students. This is not the time to overdo new initiatives or undergo long-range thinking. Everything at this point is abstract. We don't know who will be in our classrooms and how the dynamics will unfold. My suggestion is to keep the beginning of the year for developing routines, building relationships, and getting to know where we are academically.

STEP 2 – September and October are when reality sets in. We spend weeks with our students and get to know their academic and social interaction styles. Now is the time to start looking at student data, and developing plans to reach all of our learners. This is also the time when teachers start feeling the "new" falling away. I like to use September and October to provide not only data discussions but also to participate in social activities with staff to put some fun into this part of the year.

STEP 3 – Then, we get to the months of November and December. As we get closer to the holidays you would think schools would be full of joy and goodwill. In my experience, this is not true. Think about it. The weather is starting to turn colder. The days are getting shorter due to daylight savings time. With the holidays comes more spending, more eating, schedules that change from the usual, planning dinners, and special events such as concerts and holiday parties, our people are stretched to the limit. At this time of year, it is best to keep school events and activities at a reasonable level so our staff can stay engaged.

STEP 4 – January is a pivotal month. The new year brings new possibilities. It also brings New Year's resolutions. This is not the time to provide a sumptuous breakfast. My suggestion is to provide fun, active experiences for the staff. One year, we held a staff painting party, and one time, we went bowling. We had a blast as a staff right when it was needed.

And here is a special note about the third Monday in January. That day is what's known as blue Monday. It's the day when holiday bills start rolling in, and New Year's resolutions start rolling out. Make an intentional effort to be uplifting and encouraging to your staff. This is the time to provide a mid-winter tea and cookies cart, a hot chocolate bar, or maybe arrange for a local company to provide chair massages.

STEP 5 – February and March are some of the lowest morale periods at school. Spring is still not quite here, and there are no major holidays until spring break rolls around. This is also the time that students tend to make the most progress academically. Use this time to drop in some special, low-key events to keep up your spirits. At my school, this is when we do family events like game night and spa night. We also do our annual cooking contest in March right before spring break.

STEP 6 – After spring break and through the end of the year is the testing season. There is no getting around that. Staff members may be more on edge as testing approaches, but if you plan some fun in this period, you can help lighten the mood. I wrote earlier about Staff Olympics and encourage this type of event if you plan it well with the engagement of staff members. We have also done a staff family feud event and pre-testing tailgate parties for our students. Moving the focus away from testing shows that you are confident that your staff have been working hard to prepare students all year, and don't need to cram at the last minute. Be cognizant, however, of the approach your staff prefers for pre-testing rituals.

STEP 7 – And now, finally, it's May and June! Time to celebrate all of your accomplishments and complete what I like to call the Summing Up. Encourage your staff to have fun with Field Day, family picnics and dances, and of course graduation or moving-on events. Intentionally planning time to reflect and look forward is essential to bringing closure to the school year.

WHAT COULD POSSIBLY GO WRONG?

The calendar is dictated by the school district.

There are elements of the annual school calendar that we cannot control. State and district testing dates, school holidays, and professional development days are just some examples. A real problem with trying to build your annual school calendar involves working around these major blocks of time. Using these calendar planning strategies actually gives you the greatest advantage in mitigating the effects of the planned big events. One example is that when testing weeks are imminent it is probably not a great idea to plan big community events at the same time. You run the risk of over-extending your staff at a time when they are most likely to be tired and focused on a specific goal.

When planning your annual calendar you should always begin with these big blocks first, and be especially aware of what you plan during the week before one of these blocks. Like it or not, the school district/state calendar overrules your school events calendar. However, you can develop your calendar more effectively when you look at the big picture of how these blocks affect your staff.

We don't have flexibility in our daily schedule due to pull out support program times.
This pushback is one we frequently encounter at the elementary school level. Students who receive services outside of their main classroom can miss valuable and required core instruction if the pullout schedules are not aligned with the general education schedule. Students who leave for things like Speech, RTI, Dyslexia, or Gifted and Talented. need to be able to access the full general education curriculum. Add to that the fact that it seems that just about every elementary school teacher who makes their own schedule likes to have their Language Arts and Reading period in the morning, and you can see how difficult it is to schedule pullout services!

Overcoming this issue requires some flexibility, and some give and take. One excellent group of teachers I knew solved this issue by adjusting their general education schedule three times per year. They would move the core subject areas to different parts of the day so that students would have different core subjects first in the day at different times during the year. This seems like it would negatively affect the pull out schedule, but it actually helped students have a more balanced effect from being pulled out of classes (when you looked at the whole school year).

Meetings are ineffective and we should never meet/ Emails are impersonal and we should always meet.
Communication is huge in all areas of our profession, and we must make sure we balance different needs and preferences in how we communicate with our staff. We have all been in a meeting that we believed could have been an email. But we cannot make that generalization for every staff member. Some people need to hear it to understand. Some people have questions that provide greater clarity even for those staff members who thought they already understood what was going on. To be clear, not every bit of information has to be disseminated in a meeting, and most administrivia can be handled by email. However, those people who need to hear information to understand should be given the option of meeting in person (or via interactive video) if they need that format.

We run the real risk of isolating our staff members if we never meet in person, or at least via interactive video. The teaching profession can be extremely isolated for those teachers who close their room doors and do the work without much interaction with other adults. And while it is definitely preferable to send out the schedule for early release day lunches via email, we probably want to discuss the progress of initiatives in person.

It's not fair to let people choose their duty.
Having been in education for 40 years, I have gone through many seasons of life. When I became a principal for the first time my older two children were six months and two years old. With my wife and I both being Texas transplants, we did not have extended family to help us care for the kids (including the third one we had five years later). The kids

went to daycare which required a morning and afternoon trip that depended on the daycare's hours. My point in relating this common tale is that in those days, our before and after school time was much more limited than it became later.

When we consider teacher and staff needs in relation to the duty schedule, we run the risk of appearing to favor one group of staff over another. Some people can always do morning duty or may prefer to come early. Some can more easily do afternoon duty or may be able to stay later. While we may not be able to accommodate every preference, it goes a long way to creating a culture that values our staff if we at least explore the possibility of using staff input as we develop our duty schedules.

A PERSPECTIVE FROM THE FIELD

Dr. Hope Weinberg, District Supervisor of Literacy and Learning, New York

A calendar is only as successful as the teacher who remembers the dates and special events!

The Wonderful World of Weekly Memos

Over the course of the day, educators are expected to teach math, read books, tie sneakers, call parents, handle a kickball conflict, apply band-aids and sharpen hundreds of pencils. How can they ALSO be expected to remember what it says on the calendar for the events of the week ahead!

No matter how many times we send out a save-the-date, share a calendar of events, or paste a hard copy in a common area, we WILL forget something! We are human, and this will happen! However, no one wants to be the only teacher missing the Fire Prevention Assembly. Or the teacher who didn't know about the monthly meeting regarding a new curricular initiative.

Teachers are busy, administrators are busy, and we are all trying to manage it successfully and with a smile.

I remember back to my first year as a teacher – creating a beautiful, color-coordinated weekly newsletter, with a cute and catchy newsletter title. The Teacher Times highlighted what my students were learning, contained some friendly reminders for upcoming events and even included a calendar of events. I didn't know then the impact that it would have down the road as I moved into my administrative role.

One of the best ways to ensure that members of my school community are aware of upcoming events is with the idea of a weekly memo. I have seen and been through many versions of this idea.

These include:
- *Interactive calendars using a cloud-based system*
- *Narrative emails*
- *Newsletter format*
- *Bulleted list*

Over the years, I have found that the most successful method of communicating and reminding has been with a newsletter! Many of my faculty and staff members have shared that they print out their weekly newsletters and have it posted in their classrooms either next to their desks or at a commonplace in the classroom.

Aspects of the newsletters include:
- *An inspirational quote or infographic*
- *Curricular spotlights*
- *Upcoming event reminders (including a month at a glance which helps for planning)*
- *A weekly calendar of the events happening for the week ahead (a crowd favorite)*

As Martin Silverman notes, "In education, we don't have control over many things, but we do have control over time." My hope is that easing the lift of remembering dates and creating access for all who might need a gentle reminder, might save you some time searching through the multiple schedules and calendars and give you more time with your students or even self!

PLANNING THE CALENDAR - A REAL-LIFE EXAMPLE

The day I was offered my first principal position, I drove out to the school at the invitation of the Assistant Superintendent and was met by my phenomenal secretary, Helen. I asked Helen to provide me with a staff list, a handbook, and the class schedules so I could begin to learn my way around. When I looked at the schedules, I was flabbergasted. All students switched classes at least twice per day for Reading and Math. Each grade level had a different bell schedule, but all the bells rang throughout the entire school. As a matter of fact, while I was there I heard at least five bells within the first 90 minutes of the visit. I tried to understand why this would be. I asked Helen, and she told me that was "how it was set up" by the administration and that the teachers knew which bell to listen for (the bells all sounded the same). I met a teacher soon after that first visit and asked about the schedule. She told me that honestly there were so many bells that they stopped listening to them and relied on the clock to tell them when it was time to move students.

Of all the things I needed to do to make my first principalship successful, I knew that one of the top priorities had to be fixing that schedule. I soon learned in my talks with teachers that this schedule had been implemented at the suggestion of a few teachers who seemed to have some clout with the previous principal. Here is an example of how the first-grade schedule looked when I arrived there:

7:30-8:00 - Get ready for the day, unpack backpacks
8:00-8:30 - Morning Message/Social Studies
8:30-9:20 - Switch classes for Math

9:20-10:00 - TV/Movie Time (back in homeroom)
10:00-10:30 - Morning Recess
10:30-11:15 - Switch classes for Reading
11:15 -11:45 - Lunch
11:45-12:30 - Switch classes for Reading
12:30-1:15 - Switch classes for Math
1:15-1:35 - PM Recess
1:35-2:05 - Story Time/Science
2:05-2:30 - Prepare for Dismissal
2:30 - Dismissal

I had to do something.

I got together with some teachers to talk about what was important for their students. They told me they needed to learn to read well and to know basic math concepts. Some of them believed that it was best to separate students by their performance levels so that the teacher could focus on one group of students and not have to scatter their instruction across levels. While this might seem to make some sense, they also discussed how pushing kids to do more was not "developmentally appropriate." I asked them how they would get students to grow levels if they never exposed them to on-level (or above-level) work. As we talked about growing student capacity, they came to the conclusion on their own that they probably needed to have less switching during the day and keep their kids in the room so they could really know them and their learning habits better.

You'll also notice in the example I presented that there were 40 minutes of TV/Movie time. I asked about this practice and was told that they did this because "kids don't get the opportunity to see movies very much" in their lives. I found out that this period was put in the schedule a decade or so before I started there and was intended for educational programming from PBS and instructional films. In discussion, the teachers realized that this period evolved into putting in a vaguely educational video that even they admitted did not hold the students' attention. TV/Movie time was eliminated in exchange for additional Science and Social Studies instruction.

Ultimately (and quickly), the schedule was completely redone with the needs of both the students and the teachers in mind. We learned that all procedures needed to be reconsidered and revisited on a regular basis to ensure that we were using our time and resources efficiently. When the focus shifted from "we've always just done this" to "this is what we need to do" it allowed us to take control of our time and fit in all the things we needed to do!

A FINAL THOUGHT ON CALENDAR PLANNING

In education, we don't have control over many things, but we do have control over time. While we are given a calendar that contains around 180 student contact days, the content of those days is pretty much up to us. We are also given daily hours that range from 6 to 8 hours and have few limitations when it comes to finding things to fill up those hours. Since time is a precious commodity, we can and should be mindful of the balance between trying to get everything done and overdoing ourselves and our staff. When we look at making the schedule work for teachers, staff, students, and families we need to be reflective about what we do and the impact it has on our people. Less is not always more, but more is also not always more.

Finding a balance, understanding the rhythm of the school year, and maximizing opportunities while minimizing distractions are our best bets for making a great schedule. The ultimate goal is not only student success. It is also making sure we help the adults succeed so they choose to stay with us for the long haul.

CHAPTER 4
CREATING A CULTURE OF YES
Growth Mindset and the Power of Letting Go

*"Everything in the world began with a yes.
One molecule said yes to another molecule,
and life was born."*
~Clarice Lispector

WHEN AN ORGANIZATION BEGINS WITH "NO," WE CREATE A SPACE WHERE INNOVATION AND GROWTH ARE STIFLED

My first principalship was a dream come true. After working for seven years as a teacher and three as a teacher appraiser and assistant principal in wonderful, difficult, inner-city schools in Houston and San Antonio, I was given the opportunity to be the principal of a PK-2nd grade school of 425 students in a small town about 15 miles outside of San Antonio. There was no direct state accountability in those grades, the staff was very stable, and the superintendent was a former Kindergarten teacher who understood early childhood education. It was a great place to begin a career as a principal!

Once I was hired, I learned that there were some real equity issues in our school and district that the new superintendent (I was her first administrative hire) was charged with rectifying. Most pressing was the fact that the student body was approximately 50% Latino and 50% White, and a student performance gap in double digits existed between the two subgroups. We had a huge disparity in economics as well. Deep, generational rural poverty, some generational agricultural wealth and stability, a small, growing, suburban middle class, a neighborhood that had just recently gotten running water where people lived in houses, travel trailers, and many different housing structures in between.

There was a pervasive notion among a large majority of my staff that some students came to school wanting to learn, and others didn't. On the surface, this was difficult to combat at first. Empirical evidence showed that the more well-off kids did their homework, read at higher levels, and behaved better in class than the less well-off. I was 31 and a new principal, coming from schools where families struggled economically, but were given support by the school to help their children progress academically and socially. Being young and impatient, I made the rookie mistake of blowing out a bunch of things we could do to fix this issue. The common response from the staff was a resounding "no."

CREATING A CULTURE OF YES IN YOUR ORGANIZATION

As a parent and educator, my goal is to build capacity and encourage students, staff, and the community to internalize their successes and analyze their areas for growth (followed by action) to make improvements. There are not many things scarier as a parent than to have your child come up with ideas that you know could potentially be fraught with pitfalls, but you let them try them out anyway. *A note of explanation as we begin exploring this idea: I am not talking about allowing dangerous, illegal, immoral, or unethical ideas to go ahead with a yes.* I still tell my 25-year-old son that buying a motorcycle for commuting is a terrible idea. Luckily, his wife agrees and tells him no for me.

This chapter is intended to help you build a culture of innovation and self-actualization for staff, students, and the community. It is often easier to say no when someone has an idea, wants to make a change, or challenges a deeply-held tradition. But we need to be able to change our mindset to start with yes first so we can create a culture that honors growth and keeps staff members motivated to stick around.

How Do I Begin to Create a Culture of "Yes"?

The ideas in this chapter will help you to improve your practice and also build the kind of culture that makes people want to stay at your school. They may require a change in mindset and a commitment to taking a deep breath before acting on a situation. Some of us, especially those of us who are also parents, tend to begin with "no" when asked to do something outside our comfort zones (see the motorcycle example). Saying no to an idea that seems different, off, outlandish, or work-heavy is a natural response. Sometimes, no is the absolutely correct answer when handling a new idea. However, we need to consider where ideas generate and how. Staff members who are looking at a problem in a different way and, more importantly, with a different perspective need to be heard.

Consider different perspectives when considering a request or proposal: At one point, I was sitting in my office with a leadership team member discussing some planning for the next school year. She was telling me about an idea she had for building some time into the master schedule for student interest activities. She proposed a change in the master schedule that would switch specials period times (Music, PE, STEAM) for different grade levels. I mentioned this to one of the specials teachers, and she had a strong response advocating for leaving the schedule as it was in the past school year. The leadership team member was irritated that the suggestion was met with resistance.

I offered this analogy in response, which is one of the actions I believe all leaders need to consider when dealing with requests and proposals. I told her that from where I was sitting in the office I could see behind her out the window and know who was passing by, what the weather was like, and wonder why that school bus made three loops around the entry circle just now. From her perspective at the conference table, she could see the whiteboard behind me with the list of things we needed to consider for next year, and see out the office door to know who was waiting to talk to me next. I told her the perspective we needed to have was from above, where we could see all the pieces working together and get a big-picture view of the situation.

Another way to look at this is to have what is called a "balcony view" of what is going on in the school. When leaders are always on the ground, it's difficult to see what is beyond the next person or around the next curve. It's important to get a perspective from above the action to help us better evaluate how decisions fit into the bigger picture of our organization.

Create a one-question survey to send with your weekly staff communication that asks, "What is something you need to make your classroom run more effectively?" You can use the results of this survey in the short term by doing some of the items immediately. If it's supplies, purchase them. If it's support, provide it. You can also use the responses to create longer term solutions by planning to delegate resources or updating procedures.

Consider saying yes even if it scares you: When I first arrived at the most recent school I worked in, there was a leadership culture that could be defined as being hesitant to take risks. In my first few weeks at the school, I noticed that one grade level was out together at recess except for one class that had a substitute teacher. I asked the substitute why she wasn't outside with the rest of the classes. She told me she had been a sub at our school for years and that the "rule" was that subs were not allowed to take students out to recess.

My first reaction was disbelief, but I followed that by trying to understand why that procedure was in place. I figured that there may have been an issue with a sub not supervising a class. Or maybe it was because you needed a key to get back into the building and subs only received a classroom key. Whatever the reason may have been, I talked to several staff members about this situation. They were all in agreement that a substitute should be able to take a class to recess with everyone else, and that became the new procedure.

It may be difficult to let go of a procedure or idea that has been in place for a long time, but even if we are worried about what could happen if we implement change, we cannot allow that fear to be what determines our path forward.

Avoid "Yes, but…" whenever possible: This is a difficult habit to break. Nothing makes a person happier than having one of their carefully considered ideas or proposals approved. If we are building our teachers into the type of leaders that are committed to our schools and who want to stay with us for a long time, we need to create a culture where we demonstrate that we trust their judgment. Sometimes, in seeking to understand a proposal or idea we listen to someone tell us what they want to do or change. Then, we say to them, "Yes, but..." and give a list of reasons why something is too difficult: costs too much to implement or doesn't fit with the direction we are going. In this example, yes, but... is not a yes at all. It is a no wrapped in pretty paper.

This is not to say that we should always immediately say yes to every idea brought to us. Rather than get into the habit of saying yes, but... we should frame our clarifying questions to allow the person to communicate their ideas and purpose without sounding like we are agreeing to not agree.

You don't need to fix everything: I will freely admit that this step is often difficult for me. Having been in education for a multitude of years, I found myself wanting to solve every problem and provide solutions for so many of the issues that came my way. Teachers that worked with me knew one of my expectations was that if you came to me with a problem I expected you would also come to me with a suggestion for a solution. This was not always practical of course, but at the very least, I expected you to come to me with a vision of what a resolution would look like.

From my experience, I found that my big-picture view of our school could usually help frame a solution that worked for everyone. However, I was not trying to create a culture where issues were solved outside the place where they existed. Trying to fix all the problems stifles the culture of yes because it serves to stifle the questions that will lead to organic solutions right at the source of the issue.

A STEP-BY-STEP APPROACH TO CREATE THE CULTURE OF YES

STEP 1 – Use your two ears and two eyes before you use your one mouth

We have all been given this advice: We are given two ears and only one mouth so that we can listen twice as much as we speak. School administrators (and teachers) are often Type A personalities are used to constantly doing, constantly fixing, and constantly acting in situations, and our ability to reflect is often not as strongly evolved. We believe we know the right thing to do in almost every situation. But when we take the time to listen to other perspectives on an issue and truly consider that input, we are more likely to make a better decision.

Our school district participates in a staff survey process that is administered externally through our state association for school boards. The survey results are shared with the district and the campuses, and we are asked to create plans to improve in areas where our positive responses are lowest. Questions such as, "Would you recommend your school to a friend as a good place to work?" or "I can communicate honestly with my supervisor." give us great insight on how we listen and communicate.

In addition, survey questions such as, "What is working well at our school that we need to continue?" help us understand if we are nurturing a culture of yes or if we are stifling growth in our staff. Ask, observe, and listen before you tell.

STEP 2 – Go for it

Some people love extreme sports, climbing mountains, or skydiving. I am not one of those people. It is very easy for someone to suggest that we just go for things, but for those of us who are risk-averse, that is often a difficult concept! While considering saying yes to a new idea can be scary, we have to be willing to accept potential blowback. It would be foolish to ignore real risks, but it is also foolish to attempt to bubble-wrap our plans to avoid any potential negative consequences.

Providing space for staff members to think and consider ideas is crucial to our success. One of the best ways to do this is by providing dedicated thinking time in our school calendars for this purpose. To accomplish this, one option is to flip our traditional PLC time and create a reflective practice space. At one school I worked in, we did this by having a schedule on certain days where groups of staff met for two-hour blocks to consider a problem of practice based on observed actions. One example was that the administration and teachers wondered if students working in independent workstations were really engaged and meeting the intended criteria. During our two-hour reflective time, we discussed how stations should look and what the intended outcomes would be. Then, we spent time observing each other's classrooms to see what students were actually doing in stations while the teacher was working with small groups. We took that data back to the table and developed plans to enhance our communication of expectations to students and to monitor their work more effectively.

While I still think jumping out of an airplane is insanity, I believe that one of the best things we can do for our staff is to allow them the space to think, dream, and conceptualize their ideas into workable plans. We all know that people stay where they are valued, and where their ideas are considered. Sometimes, we need to jump out of that plane, and just go for it.

STEP 3 – Eliminate the qualifiers to Yes

Following Step 2 with Step 3 is one of the most important elements in creating a culture of yes in our schools. We've taken the time to listen. We've developed ideas for implementing new processes together. And now we are considering how to actually move into the action stage of implementation. Yes, but... is one of the most limiting phrases when we are trying to get staff to buy into our culture. Nothing seems more false than saying we encourage input and innovation and then stifling action with qualifiers.

To be clear, we can't say yes to every idea. There are some real limitations to implementing certain ideas (think budget, time, ability to manage). There is a difference between putting limitations on an idea and denying it outright. If we are doing the work correctly, ideas for innovation come from observable and measurable data. A problem has been identified, and we are utilizing our staff resources to solve that problem. In the brainstorming sessions we have already completed, we accepted and rejected different ideas. Now is the time to take action knowing what the potential pitfalls may be.

Here's an example: One year, during an after-school cooking club for boys, I asked the group this question. "If we could provide additional drink options other than water or milk for lunch, what would be a good option?" The responses varied from soda to fruit juice, to lemonade (as well as some truly weird stuff). I explained that we had to follow health guidelines first, so we were never going to choose soda as an option. This was not a Yes, but… It was a flat-out No. My point is that by only considering actionable options we create a clear path to yes. The same process needs to happen in our interactions with staff members as we create solutions to problems of practice.

STEP 4 – Allow solutions to come from those who do the work

It has been 30+ years since I have been a classroom teacher. One or two things may have changed in our profession over that period, and I cannot consider myself to be an expert in teaching at this point. I relate this to my appreciation for music. When I was in seventh grade, I played the tenor saxophone in the junior high band. I haven't played an instrument since. While I listen to and appreciate music, I am not a direct practitioner and consider myself to be more of a supporter and fan of the talented musicians who bring that joy to our lives.

As a parent, my adult children still ask for advice on life, and would often appreciate a direct answer to the question, "What should I do about…?" It is my role to provide insight and guidance, but I don't live their lives and most importantly don't feel the direct consequences of their decisions. The same goes for teachers in the classroom. Teachers often ask for solutions to their issues such as discipline problems, instructional situations, and dealing with parents. It would be very easy for us as school leaders to just tell them what to do. However, we are not the ones that have to implement or experience the consequences. Real problem-solving will occur when we advise and assist the practitioners who have the insight and direct knowledge to make things happen in their classrooms and our schools.

As an administrator, I have worked with several teachers who were having a difficult time managing behavior and organizing instruction in their classrooms. When I was early in my career, I knew the solution was to show them how to create an organizational system that would provide needed structure. The mistake I made was to think that by either giving them a system to implement or showing them a master teacher who had one implemented they would be able to replicate it in their classrooms. What I didn't realize was that unless they saw how and why the systems were developed and implemented they could not replicate them effectively. There were so many steps that preceded implementation and being told to do it virtually guaranteed that it would not be done well.

A PERSPECTIVE FROM THE FIELD

Barb Schwamann
Superintendent of Schools, Iowa
Building staff buy-in and fostering strong relationships in an educational setting is crucial for creating a positive, collaborative, and effective learning environment, what we have deemed a Culture of Yes. These strategies have been crucial in enhancing staff morale, promoting professional growth, and ultimately

benefiting student outcomes in the two rural school districts I have served. Here's why these elements are essential for a positive YES culture.

BUILDING STAFF BUY-IN

Creates Ownership and Commitment: *When staff members feel included in decision-making and are part of shaping the school's mission and vision, they are more likely to be committed to the goals and objectives of the school. Buy-in generates ownership, which leads to motivation and accountability.*

Promotes Innovation and Risk-Taking: *Staff members who are invested in the school's vision are more willing to innovate and take risks in their teaching, knowing their contributions are valued and supported.*

Reduces Resistance to Change: *Involving staff in changes, such as curriculum updates or policy shifts, helps reduce resistance. When teachers are part of the process, they understand the reasoning behind decisions and are more likely to support them.*

BUILDING RELATIONSHIPS

Fosters Trust and Respect: *Strong relationships between staff members, and between staff and leadership, build trust. Trust creates a culture where educators feel supported, valued, and more willing to collaborate.*

Increases Collaboration and Teamwork: *When teachers have good relationships with each other, it fosters collaboration, sharing of resources, and the exchange of ideas, which benefits the entire school community.*

Improves Morale and Job Satisfaction: *Healthy relationships lead to a positive work environment, reducing stress and increasing job satisfaction. This can lead to better teacher retention rates and a more cohesive staff.*

BEING AVAILABLE AND LISTENING TO STAFF

Demonstrates Support and Care: *Being physically and emotionally available shows staff that leadership cares about their well-being. It signals that their voices matter, which encourages open communication.*

Builds Open Communication: *By actively listening to staff concerns, ideas, and suggestions, leaders foster an open communication culture. This leads to a more engaged and involved staff.*

Informs Decision-Making: *Listening to staff provides leaders with valuable insights into the real challenges teachers face. This can inform decisions that more accurately meet the needs of the school community.*

VISIBILITY IN CLASSROOMS

Builds a Culture of Support: *Leaders who regularly visit classrooms demonstrate that they are invested in the daily activities of the school. Visibility reassures teachers that they are supported and recognized for their efforts.*

Provides Real-Time Insights: *Regular classroom visits allow leaders to observe teaching practices, student engagement, and classroom dynamics. This first-hand knowledge helps leaders make informed decisions about professional development and resources.*

Strengthens Relationships with Students and Staff: *When school leaders are visible and approachable, it fosters stronger relationships with both students and teachers. It shows staff that leadership is present, aware, and involved in the school's instructional mission.*

Building staff buy-in, fostering strong relationships, being available, and being visible are key to creating a positive and effective school culture. With these actions, leaders can create a foundation for trust and collaboration. This leads to a shared sense of purpose, enhanced collective efficacy, and improved student outcomes. A supportive, inclusive environment ensures that staff members feel valued, motivated, and empowered to contribute their best, creating a thriving educational setting.

WHAT COULD POSSIBLY GO WRONG?

Just tell me what you want me to do.

If you read educational theory and look at educational social media you might be led to believe that everyone in our profession wants to have input into every policy and procedure at our schools. In my practice, I find this to be untrue. Educators make hundreds of decisions every day, and quite honestly, some people are tired of it. Remembering that not everyone is interested in every bit of what we do is important because some educators just want to be told what to do in specific situations. When we constantly ask them to participate in the development of dress code, the scheduling of interventions, or the timing of school events, we risk staff members getting bogged down in the minutiae of administrivia and they are less able to focus their attention on what matters most to them.

Some decisions just need to be made by administrators and be done with them. An easy method of getting voluntary input from interested parties is to simply offer a one-question survey such as, "If you have any input or ideas for developing the daily schedule, please indicate them below." Those who want to input can, and those who don't are not obligated to participate in the process.

That won't work because…

Nothing is more frustrating than working diligently and collaboratively on a plan for success and then presenting it to staff who pick it apart for what might happen. "The parents will never go for that. You'll have so many complaints." Or, "The district won't support that. Where's the money going to come from?" We've all heard these questions when presenting a plan of action. These may seem like they come from a place of negativity, but what I've found is that they usually come from a place of anxiety and fear. Change is not easy, and what we've always done is usually more comfortable than what we might do.

Making the planning process open and available to observers who don't want to participate can often help limit this type of pushback. They are not required to do the planning work if they don't want to, but they can listen to how the plans were developed so they understand the why of what is being implemented. In addition, communication during planning and implementation is key to building an understanding of the process along with the product.

You're Not Listening to What I'm Saying.
Sometimes, requests come to us in a totally different language than what is intended. A staff member who complains of being tired or overworked might prompt you to find out if they're sleeping OK or if there's something going on in their personal life that is making them feel that way. What does tired actually mean? We often find out that describing feelings before identifying a problem is pretty common. However, with a school to run and being pulled in so many directions, we often find ourselves doing things to alleviate a symptom without figuring out what is causing the problem to begin with.

Using the example of being told that someone is tired requires us to understand that these symptoms often come from people who ARE truly tired. Tired of being told what to do and how to do it. Tired of thinking about improvement and being told no when they propose a solution. Let's be clear. You will tell people no, and people will tell you no. But listening to what people are really saying by considering the source of their questions and concerns helps us focus on true issues and build strong school culture by maximizing our ability to say yes.

That's easy for you to say...
Perspective in our profession is everything. Consider my saying from earlier: While decisions are often made by people that work on carpet, they are implemented by people that work on tile. Plans made in a vacuum that don't include perspective from the people who have to do the work are not set up to be successful. The people that have to actually implement decisions know how logistics will work. They can often see the potential pitfalls more clearly than those of us outside the area of direct contact with students. It's easy for us to tell someone to do something and easy for us to say no when they want to change a procedure. How often have you thought about someone who left the classroom or school setting and "forgot what it's like here in the trenches"?

Saying yes is sometimes just as easy as saying no. When we resolve to build a culture of yes, we recognize that sometimes the expert in a situation is not us. Building capacity to affect change is worthwhile and will definitely improve school culture. We just need to be prepared for the time when the ideas that flow from us to those who do the work are met with a less enthusiastic response.

CREATING A CULTURE OF YES IN REAL LIFE
At the beginning of this chapter, I described what greeted me as I began my first principalship in a school that needed a culture refresh. The teachers and staff at that school were

incredible people. There was little question that there was a desire to provide a positive environment for children to grow in even though there were some important issues that needed to be resolved to adjust the culture and change practices that were entrenched. The previous administration was what could be described as old-school and paternal. There are some amazing benefits of that style, but innovation was not encouraged in that culture.

Once we confronted the need to provide equitable opportunity for all the students at that school, a group of teachers cautiously agreed to join me in looking for effective programs and practices we could implement to improve our practice. As a primary, grade-focused school we were able to laser focus on early childhood practices that were proven to be effective. During that time there was research being done on multi-age classroom structures that mixed students of different ages and grade levels in one classroom similar to the "one-room schoolhouse" idea. A group of teachers and I read about multi-age and decided we wanted to look into this idea further.

The school had about 8-10 teachers per grade level at the time. Studying the multi-age program was open to all staff but not required. About 15 teachers and I met and read articles about multi-age implementations locally and across the world. We found a local area school that had been implementing this structure for a few years, and we visited as a group and talked to the administrators and teachers. We considered which grades could participate effectively, and how students and parents would be affected. There was so much synergy in the discussions, and ideas from the doable to the outlandish were thrown around. There were many yes moments and also a few no moments as well. Ultimately, the group decided that we would pilot a multi-age program in some K-2 classes. There were six teachers who committed to being the first to try it out. The teachers that did not choose to be part of the implementation were honored for their commitment to study, and there was no consequence for not participating in the pilot.

Parent meetings were held to inform and gauge interest in the pilot. Teachers who would be continuing with single-grade classrooms expressed some concern that attention and resources would be diverted from them to this new program and had to be assured that the idea was to provide choice to parents and teachers so we could best serve our students. Because of the extensive planning from the committee, our district was fully supportive of this innovation. Classrooms were selected, furniture was adjusted, schedules were created, and we even had a local cabinet maker create a collapsible table space in the hallway for small group instruction.

We implemented this program the following fall semester, and the teachers did a phenomenal job explaining and owning the philosophy and practice of multi-age grouping. Parents were excited to have options, and I even put my own two kids in that program when they were in those grades. The teachers had a renewed sense of purpose and belonging which led them to commit the rest of their careers to that school and district. All but one of the teachers is now retired, but they all stayed because they experienced the culture of yes.

A FINAL THOUGHT ON CREATING A CULTURE OF YES

We are told that the best school culture we can create is one where students are seen, valued, and heard. This goes for staff members as well. Creating a culture of yes involves seeing staff for their individual perspectives and talents, valuing their input and creativity, and hearing their concerns, dreams, and aspirations for the school. When we create a culture that values innovation and expression we validate the fact that while we know a lot, we don't know everything. People want to work where their input is valued and appreciated. Once our staff know that our default value is yes rather than no, they are more likely to feel part of the work of our schools and much more likely to stay with our organization!

CHAPTER 5
ONE SIZE DOES NOT FIT ALL
Creating a Culture for All Sizes

"Intentional leadership is being self-aware and knowing that our teams are not one-size-fits-all."
~Kerry Alison Wekelo

WE SPEND TOO MUCH TIME DELIVERING OUR MESSAGE TO THE GREAT MIDDLE INSTEAD OF CONSIDERING INDIVIDUAL NEEDS

There is no way around the fact that I am not the kind of person that fits the one-size-fits-all clothing ideal. I am way taller than standard, my head is larger than most, I am rounder in some places, and less round in others. I dread finding a shirt I like that fits most people, but is way too short for me and won't tuck into my trousers. Caps that have those holes to resize in the back are straining at the first hole when I put them on my head. It's just a fact of life for me, and it makes me think about how group-think in education is one reason staff members often choose to leave.

In my first year of teaching, I taught first grade alongside a veteran teacher who had been teaching first grade for 30 years at that time. It occurred to me that she was essentially doing the same job as I was in my first year, but she was much more adept at making things happen for her students than I was at that point. We attended the same meetings, the same professional development sessions, and were held to the same standards. There was no expectation of her or of me to be any more effective or more efficient with our classes. However, she was at a very different place in her ability and career. Even then, I realized that considering us to be the same was likely not an effective method to grow me or to sustain her.

If it has not already become clear to those of us in school leadership, the time to standardize our staff has long passed. We continually coach our teachers to be flexible and meet the varying needs of our students without doing the same thing ourselves for our staff members. Creating a culture that considers the variety of teachers in our schools is key to building capacity as well as providing a stimulating work environment that will both challenge and celebrate our people. And when you are challenged and celebrated, you want to stay part of that organization. This includes consideration of their talents, abilities, personality, culture, and motivation among other traits.

As an example, I believe that many school leaders, myself included, have honorable intentions when it comes to designing teacher professional development. If we consider the fact that we sometimes roll out new initiatives, it would seem at surface level that we should throw all the information out to everyone at the same time in the same way. I have experienced this type of professional development as both a consumer and a provider. Literacy Program 101 is one of the most popular courses in the elementary PD repertoire. At its essence though, this type of training is really not intended to meet the needs of any but the great middle of end-users. Our standardized thinking compels us to think that everyone needs every bit of the information when we know that some people are already far beyond the beginning stages of this, or any implementation.

ONE SIZE DOES NOT FIT ALL

When we consider the fact that our staff, just like our student body, is composed of people with varying needs, talents, abilities, and motivations, we can design opportunities to meet their needs more closely. One of the greatest concerns that teachers express is the fact that their abilities are not considered when they attend a meeting or professional development session. This seems like a lot of work, but just as we expect our teachers to meet student needs, we are charged with meeting staff needs as well. I will argue the fact that you will ultimately save time as you will no longer need to target a message, and then follow up with reinforcement for those who need it and challenges for those who don't. There are many elements to consider when we put these strategies into action. Here are some things you can do right now.

How Do I Begin Differentiating for Staff?

Plan for the receiver, not the presenter. When you are planning a meeting or professional development session, shift the focus from the content of your message to the needs of the receivers. Understand that you know what you are trying to convey, but your audience will consist of people that will instantly get it and make connections, along with others who will not see the meaning or value of what you say. When you speak from a place of understanding, you can tailor the message to the audience. You may not need everyone to sit through a full day of information, while others may need the day plus a follow-up session.

Consider what motivates people and build that into your messages. As a leader and consumer of professional development, I enjoy a good ice-breaker. However, I am not blind to the eye-rolling and sneering of my colleagues and staff whenever this type of activity is presented. As leaders, we need to consider different preferences and plan for reaching our people in different ways. Communication styles and preferences, movement, recognition, and participation all should be considered when working with our staff members.

Beware of microaggressions. Even with the best intentions and a strong desire to provide equity and honor to all people, we sometimes perpetuate ideas and systems that are inherently inequitable. For example, it is common for schools to ask staff members to participate in step counting challenges or weight-loss competitions. These are almost always voluntary, but for staff members who are physically challenged, on medications that prevent this activity, suffer from eating disorders, or who are already fit, challenges such as this provide a sense of division from the organization. I am not suggesting that we eliminate all events that are not achievable by everyone. I merely recommend that consideration be taken to provide and communicate the fact that a multitude of events are available and that everyone has the opportunity to participate at some point. Think to add rather than subtract opportunities for people to be involved and connect.

Make a list of all staff and know at least one personal fact or preference for each. This is a simple step that will yield dividends. When you make a conscious and concerted effort to know something about a person, you create a connection that not only strengthens your personal connection but also helps connect you both to the organization. One of the most revealing outcomes of this activity is finding out that you may not know something about every staff member. Set a goal to purposefully connect with any staff members that have blank spaces next to their names. Also, note that this is an excellent activity for teachers to do with a list of their students.

Be purposefully inclusive. I attended a professional development session where the participants were asked to give their thoughts about the game Musical Chairs and to tell of their experience playing that game. The group noted that if you were not quick you were often the first one out and the game was over for you until the next round. The presenter suggested a slight game modification which was to still remove one chair whenever the music stopped but to not remove a player each round. The goal of the game switched to figuring out how to get the same number of people on increasingly fewer chairs until there was only one chair left and all the players. The game shifted from a goal of exclusivity to one of inclusivity with that one modification. By being purposefully inclusive we shift the focus to allow more and different perspectives and talents to be considered.

Remember your 100% is not everyone else's 100%. Consider not only the impact but also the level of implementation for your requests and requirements. While your position or your passion might be 100% concerned with a single content area or support program, that is not the case for those who receive your information. Look at the big picture of where your message fits into the operation of the school. This helps reduce the stress teachers feel about multiple people taking multiple chunks of their time.

A STEP-BY-STEP GUIDE TO DIFFERENTIATING FOR STAFF

STEP 1 – Plan before you plan.

I might even suggest planning before you plan to plan. Every year for many years I have attended the annual summer administrator training sessions before other staff return to school and we begin campus training. Inevitably, the various required content ends up making the sessions feel like drinking from a fire hose and being bombarded with information from several directions. Because we often have several new members of the administrative team, we are often given Subject 101 refresher courses intended to ensure that all members of the group have received the basics. The sessions are planned to provide the same information in the same way to all of us regardless of our aptitude or prior understanding.

This happens with teachers as well. As school leaders, we want to ensure that everyone knows the information from the staff handbook, for example. Some staff may have heard the handbook information multiple times over multiple years, and some may be hearing it for the first time. We lose the interest and connection of staff members when we make them sit through sessions for information they already know.

If we take the time to plan before we plan these sessions, we are more able to consider the variety of needs in our audience and can better focus our messages in different ways. In both examples it would be better to plan a group connection-building activity, then strands of essential learning based on the needs of the groups.

STEP 2 – Know the love languages of your staff

Gary Chapman and Paul White wrote a book called *The 5 Languages of Appreciation in the Workplace*. This book was inspired by Dr. Chapman's work in identifying 5 Love Languages in the context of personal relationships. This adaptation with Dr. White helps us understand the different approaches that help people feel appreciated in the workplace. Using these approaches can help us know how our people feel valued at work, and we can make an effort to dispense with one-size-fits-all motivational techniques.

There is a difference between recognition and appreciation. When people are recognized for an accomplishment we often do so in public gatherings. For some people, this is embarrassing, especially if they are not the type to enjoy being the center of attention. When we appreciate people for their work we usually do this more privately and quietly. The five ways to show appreciation are: Words of Affirmation, Tangible Gifts, Quality Time, Acts of Service, and Physical Touch. Knowing our people means knowing which of these is their primary motivator. Beyond just knowing, however, we also need to consciously use these actions when dealing with our staff.

Examples of each action include:
- Words of Affirmation
    - "I really appreciate how you…"
    - "You're so great at _____."
- Tangible Gifts
    - "Here is a token of my appreciation for what you did."

- ○ "I know you collect _____, and I saw this and thought of you."
- Quality Time
  - ○ "I'd love to meet with you to talk about _____."
  - ○ "Will you join me at the meeting about _____? I'd love to get your input."
- Acts of Service
  - ○ "Can I cover your class for an hour or so? You could have some planning time."
  - ○ "Let me take this off your plate so you can focus on _____."
- Physical Touch
  - ○ "Here's a hug for having handled that so expertly."
  - ○ "Give me a high-five! You're incredible."

STEP 3 - Be cognizant of equity and avoid microaggressions

I realize this statement is said simply yet, in actuality, is quite complicated. Using an equity lens as we work is often more difficult than we realize because most of us do not intend to be inequitable. On the most basic level, educational leaders need to understand that all doesn't always mean all. For example, not all math teachers have equal skills, training, or outlook. In a group of third-grade teachers, you will have varying levels of expertise, experience, and ability to create lessons. To expect the same output from every staff member is the easiest way to ensure that your expectations will not be met.

Beyond basic equity concerns are the concerns of the humanity of our staff. Everyone comes to us with a different story, different education, and different life experiences. We can create more equitable experiences by examining our procedures to ensure they are accessible to all staff. For example, do we reward people who have the means to stay later to work on projects over the new parent that has to be home by a certain time to care for their child? Do our structures favor the outspoken or the complainer? Do we ask for input, then discount that which comes from complainers?

Avoiding microaggressions can also be tricky for leaders. Again, most of us would not deliberately insult or exclude someone, but often we don't think about how our setup creates this type of environment. Earlier, I gave the example of the workplace weight-loss challenge as a potential microaggression. Another example I can give is when we celebrate religious events with little thought given to those who are irreligious or celebrate something else. I want to be clear about the fact that I don't believe we should de-culturize our schools to the point of sterility. It is important to honor the culture of our students, staff, and community. When we choose to celebrate one culture fully and neglect, or worse, trivialize another, we are creating an environment that is not conducive to retaining staff members.

STEP 4 - Get to really know your people

As I suggested earlier, one of the easiest ways we can ensure that we know something about our staff members is to take a school roster and write a fact about each person on the list. If we don't know something about everyone, it's time to get out and communicate with staff members in general, appropriately-personal terms. We can find out where people are from. We can often connect on having attended the same (or rival) high schools or universities. We can know if staff members are connected to a significant other, children, or pets. Favorite foods, travel destinations, new homes, and hobbies are things we can know about our staff members and these help us create relationships that connect us to each other and to the organization.

If I know staff member AW likes chocolate, I will have some at meetings. Staff member CQ is a fan of sports, and I can mention the latest game when we run into each other in the hallway. This might sound trivial on the surface, but from my experience and research on employee satisfaction, people tend to stay in a place where they feel connected. A Gallup Poll on the engagement of American employees in the workplace from 2023 reported that 33% felt "more detached from their employers, with less clear expectations, lower levels of satisfaction with their organization, and less connection to its mission or purpose, than they did four years ago. They are also less likely to feel someone at work cares about them as a person." We increase that percentage by creating these connections. Use the QR code to review the full report.

STEP 5 - Get a true perspective

In my first year at one of the schools I worked in, I met a bright and enthusiastic woman who was in charge of running a grant program that was part of my school's science curriculum in fifth grade. At that time I had two teachers working with the grant directly, and I was informed that over the summer one of the teachers did not complete a required grant activity. I was told by the director that I would probably need to move her out of the grade for non-compliance. This was a classic example of perspective. When you consider that 100% of the grant director's job was this project, it made sense that she would be so laser-focused. What she didn't consider was that the grant was probably 5% of this teacher's responsibilities. And if you figured the percentage of the school as a whole, the grant was probably down in the tenths of a percent.

This example is not intended to minimize the work of people who are focused on one area. It helps all of us to have people dedicated to special education for example, who are able to dig deep into effective practices and legal issues. However, if we intend to retain our staff, we need to be aware of the fact that what is currently filling our attention may not be what is filling theirs. I liken this to a time when I was trying to eat healthier and was given a plate of delicious fudge as a gift. One bite of fudge would not do permanent damage to my plan. However, multiple one bites of fudge added up to a whole bunch of fudge, which did derail me for a time. Part of creating a place where the staff wants to stay is seeing the big picture and emphasizing the "big bites" that are most important.

A PERSPECTIVE FROM THE FIELD

Dr. Hope Weinberg, District Supervisor of Literacy and Learning, New York

Who you are influences how you lead, teach and learn.

There is an overwhelming need for belonging that takes over your identity when you join a school community. As mentioned above in Step 4, Get to really know your people! That's one of the beautiful things about education – the fact that you are bringing so many different worlds, life experiences and people into one place to reach the same goals (I hope): Keeping kids at the center of EVERYTHING WE DO! We do better for our kids, when the adults are seen, valued, heard, and feel like they belong in the school community.

It's human nature to want your voice to be heard, to want your ideas to be valued and to want those around you to have trust in who you are as a member of the community. So, why is something so valuable, often put to the wayside? There is a discomfort in letting yourself be seen in all forms, a vulnerability and risk. You bring your identity with you everywhere you go, and there is no hiding it (even though some people do). I can't take off my being-a-queer-woman coat depending on where I am. I take the risk every day to be brave and true to who I am because who I am is how I lead.

Your identity influences what you do every day. When you enter your school world it's important to remember that who you are influences how you lead, teach, and learn.

So, how can leaders provide the best learning for adults in their schools?

I offer the idea that identity work needs to be at the forefront of everything that happens in schools, especially at the start of the school year! During professional development sessions for a new group of participants, I create space for some type of identity work. Often this is in the form of talking about myself through pictures on a Google Slide. But the reality is that there is such depth to this work. I am letting people into my world, I am talking about what makes me who I am and how my life experiences shape the way in which I lead. Imagine this for your faculty, staff or even students. Do we actually know anything about them that we can connect to? Do we know what they need to thrive in your school, building or classroom?

I ground most of my work in Simon Sinek's work, Start With Why. No matter how many times I read his book, or listen to his TED talk, I always walk away with a deep self reflection of my purpose and my why. We don't often stop and think about our purpose as we walk into school every day, it becomes sort of routine and process. However, Sinek reminds us to stop and think about who we are and what we are doing everyday, sharing that "If you don't know why, you can't truly know how and what." It's important that we create space for our school community to reflect on their own why that drives each one of us.

Identity work not only creates transparency and vulnerability, but also creates a bridge to building community and forming relationships. We spend more time with our colleagues than our families, shouldn't we know who we work with? If we want to make a difference in the lives of kids, shouldn't we know why we do what we do everyday?

WHAT COULD POSSIBLY GO WRONG?

We don't have time to plan for everyone.
This is a real concern and one that is not simply solved by being told to manage your time better. We often work with teachers who say this is a problem in lesson planning. There is no denying that planning for the middle is easier, and maybe less time-intensive. I would suggest, however, that the amount of work done to adjust after the fact for the advanced and the struggling student, or in this case teacher, negates the ease of planning to the middle. If we flip the script a bit on the planning part, we may find that the extra up-front work yields bigger dividends.

We've always done things this way.
This potential pitfall belongs in every chapter of this book and every chapter of every book on educational leadership. When considering adjusting events and procedures there is a real risk that you will get pushback for not honoring tradition. The annual Christmas program is a great example. Inherently, this type of activity is positive and full of goodwill. We often throw in a mention of Hanukkah and Kwanzaa in our attempt to make the program appeal beyond the traditional cultural and religious traditions we celebrate. In reality though, we are deliberately excluding a

percentage of our community when we over celebrate one tradition rather than another.

I want to restate that I believe the way to create more equity is not to subtract from what we do but to add. Consider a full year's slate of events and ensure that equitable celebrations are part of what you do. When our staff knows that they will have their moment in the sun at some point in the year they are likely to connect with us on a stronger level and stay part of our community.

Another lens to consider is ableism. As I mentioned previously, I held the Staff Olympics where staff members would participate and compete in different games in front of the students as a fun, motivational activity. I was conscious as I planned the event to make sure nobody would get chosen to participate in an event that they were unable to perform easily. For example, anyone with a mobility issue would not get chosen for a racing event. Beyond this consideration though, I found that there were a few people who were not comfortable participating at all in front of the group. This was even true for events they could easily do physically. At the suggestion of a teacher, I changed the event to a *Family Feud* style team challenge, done indoors, and with no individual physical expectation. The game was just as fun for the students, and several staff members appreciated the fact that they did not have to do the physical activities outdoors.

Some people are guarded and don't share their personal life.

When you are compiling your list of staff and something personal about them, you may find that the reason you don't have something for someone is that they are not the type to share personal information. We all have varying comfort levels about sharing, and when someone is more guarded, we may not be able to know as much about them as we'd like. In this case, observation is key. You might notice that they prefer one content area to another in elementary grades or have a collection in their classroom. This is the kind of information you can gather to create connections without being intrusive.

The goal is not to create an uncomfortable situation. The goal is to find and create connections so that staff members feel at home in the school and choose to stay. There is a real risk when developing connections that we can appear to be overstepping boundaries, and I certainly don't advocate for that. While aiming to know something about 100% of staff we may find that we can only find out about 99.5%. This is still a long way toward creating the kind of connections that help staff members feel like part of the school.

What is important to me isn't important to my staff.
One of the traits I would most like to change about myself is my tendency to overly worry about ultimately small things at school. I can think of many instances where there was to be an activity or event taking place, and I was on the road to obsessively worrying about things like whether there would be enough water bottles or whether the floors would look nice for our visitors. To so many of the people I worked with these things were trivial, yet sometimes, they kept me up at night with worry. The point of this is that what is important to me may not be important to everyone. When considering the need to avoid a one-size-fits-all approach, I must

recognize that not only may the school's mission and vision be interpreted differently, but even the smaller details might not be universally accepted. The attempt to see through the eyes of another is worth the effort if it allows me to understand the viewpoint and perspective of others.

A PERSPECTIVE FROM THE FIELD

Brian Redmond, High School Band Director, Wyoming

Let me start this off by sharing an important detail of my professional life: I am a high school band teacher.

As a high school band teacher of nearly 20 years, I can tell you that I have lost count of the number of irrelevant professional developments I have attended at the various schools I have taught in. I can also tell you that my experience is in no way unique. If you happen to know a music teacher, you might ask them the last time they attended a PD session at their school that was designed or delivered with them in mind. For those that don't know a music teacher well enough to ask that question, I'll give you my answer - it hasn't happened.

I don't blame my principals. I don't blame our HR staff or the folks in the office of Curriculum, Instruction, and Assessment. Schools are judged based on test scores, and music isn't a tested subject matter. I get it 100%. Not to mention that every school I've taught at, big and small, have had multiple math, English, science, and history teachers, but I've only taught at one school with multiple music teachers (that's the school I'm currently at… we have two music teachers). With limited PD time available, folks have to go where they're going to get the biggest bang for their buck. Not to mention that I have yet to have a principal who has a music background. While some have been in band, choir, or theater as a student, none have ever taught the subject I teach.

Imagine, though, that you stop in a classroom to observe a teacher, and you notice that one student is left out of the lesson for whatever reason. You might say something to the teacher about it, or figure maybe that student is having an off day. Now imagine that you see the same student in classrooms over the course of multiple years, and every lesson excludes that student. Crazy, right?

I can tell you that I have attended numerous PD sessions teaching me to unpack our latest ELA standards. I can tell you that I once had a PD session where I was sent off with our PE teachers to discuss student engagement strategies that we were then going to share with the rest of the staff. Except we were never asked to share the strategies with the staff.

I certainly wouldn't expect any of my administrators to be experts in the area of music education. However, I would hope that, like one of the teachers of the student constantly left out of lessons, they might consider how they could include all the members of their classroom... er... staff.

DIFFERENTIATING FOR STAFF IN REAL LIFE

When I consider all the opportunities that exist and that have been missed in creating situations where I had the opportunity to provide a more personalized experience to my staff, there are too many to count. One of the best examples is when I started my first principalship in a small rural/suburban district outside of San Antonio, Texas. I was coming from having grown up and taught in urban schools, and though married to a farm girl from Iowa, I had little to no schema for the needs of the faculty and families I was hired to lead at that PK-2 primary school.

Coming from large urban school districts, my experience was that there were abundant resources and opportunities for professional development and an expectation to know and implement the latest initiatives from research to improve student outcomes. What I found when I began working in the smaller rural/suburban district was that professional development was not as easily accessible. I also found out that the skills necessary to work with our students were not the same skills we used in urban districts. The rural poverty was, by far, worse than anything I had experienced in the city, and the lack of readily available resources was nearly non-existent. My first inclination was to attempt to recreate the experiences of my previous districts in the new place. If you are reading this and shaking your head, you are correct in knowing that there was no way this was going to work. What was considered standard for the urban districts was not designed to meet the needs of the rural students and the development arc of the teachers I was blessed to be working with at the new school.

When I was in my Master's program I had a brilliant professor who would talk about a concept called the Circle of Ignorance. Picture a circle. Inside the circle is everything you already know. The circumference of the circle is what you know that you don't already know. Everything beyond the circumference of the circle is everything you don't even know you don't know. As you learn more, your circle of knowledge gets larger, and so does the circumference. You begin to realize that the more you know, the more you know that you DON'T know.

When I considered this concept in my first principalship, it not only sharpened my focus, it helped me understand that one of the most frustrating things for teachers is not change itself. The frustration is change moving five steps ahead of where we are now and not being able to see the steps to get to the new place. I immediately took several steps back and considered the teachers and staff I was working with and where they were in their educational practice. We started more deeply communicating about what our community needed and how we would get there.

One of the best examples of this was when we were charged with addressing a significant achievement gap between two student identity groups. It was clear to me that the gap was perpetrated through practices that were entrenched in the school system. The teachers did not create this gap through bad intentions. There was a culture present that was able to justify the achievement gap and put the cause on sources out of the school's control. It took a visit from the state to help this insulated community realize that something needed to be done. The teachers were mostly willing to improve outcomes as they loved the students and community but did not know how to make this happen.

We began looking together at some of the issues that seemed to be impeding student growth, and some teachers verbalized the thought that some students wanted to learn and other students didn't. The discipline data bore out this thinking as, not surprisingly, the group that had much lower academic performance was also the group with a greater number of discipline referrals that kept them out of class. Remember, these students were in grades PK-2, but there were stacks of disciplinary incident referrals from the previous year, mostly predicated by a relatively small group of teachers. It was clear that we had to focus on keeping all kids in class, but it took some major self-reflection to admit that maybe the problem resided in us and not the kids themselves. To be sure, there were serious issues exacerbated by poverty and social factors, but once we focused on the fact that students really wanted to be in school, it shifted the discussion to what we could do to encourage them to be fully part of our school experience.

Some teachers were focusing on positive behaviors while others seemed to be finding ways to be punitive with students. Teachers were invited to be on a committee to study ways to change the disciplinary focus of the school. The philosophy of discipline began to shift toward highlighting positive expectations and moving away from punitive practices. Teachers were initially offered the opportunity to create a classroom system to follow this philosophy as opposed to simply implementing a purchased product. The key to the ultimate success was this step. Allowing teachers the choice of how to begin was key to bringing together the understanding of how ownership of the process would lead to successful implementation. The great news is that after a year and a half of people doing their own thing, the staff chose to create a school-wide system that we successfully used for the rest of my time there. I believe that allowing them to differentiate for themselves was the key to their success.

A PERSPECTIVE FROM THE FIELD

LaKeyseah Brennan, Virtual Education Specialist, South Carolina

There have been many times I sat in a professional development meeting where the content was not appropriate for the grade level I taught, it was not relevant to the needs of my students, and it was not what I felt I needed as a teacher. I was always left feeling that I could have been doing something better with my time.

There have been times I sat in a professional development meeting where the content provided me with wonderful tools and resources, I was ready to share the information with my teacher friends or people in my department, and I was reminded why I wanted to be an English teacher. I was always left with not enough time to finish creating what I started during the professional development, and the ideas I wanted to share became the last thing to discuss in our department meeting because of more precedent information being disseminated from the district office.

I have been asked on several school or district-based surveys what I felt I needed in a professional development, but I don't seem to remember a time where I felt I received a PD that would help me grow as a teacher or that I had time to implement what I learned.

For instance, some days PD works better in the morning before school versus an after school meeting where everyone is exhausted. If I could use my lunch time to attend a 30 minute informational session versus coming into school early in the morning or staying after school, then I would like that option as well. We always hear things like "you can learn from the teacher down the hall" instead of hiring a consultant. If so, why are so many PD sessions spent on district level staff or outside companies and consultants coming in to show us how to implement direct instruction when Mrs. Robinson works with similar students upstairs in the math wing? There are teachers who are great at what they do and *would love to share with their colleagues, but is this an opportunity given to the teachers? *you will spend less money if you pay a teacher their daily rate for the session**

What if we worked together based on grade levels and created more interdisciplinary lessons where students can see what writing looks like as a historian, mathematician, or scientist, and not just through a literary lens? What if I am a ninth-grade teacher struggling with my students, how can I find time to collaborate with other ninth-grade teachers to discuss how they handle certain situations or ways we can increase student success?

I have seen cool ideas such as a menu option for PD. It is like you can feel seen or heard without speaking or seeing anyone because there are options you can access to provide you with what you need at that moment. Today, I may need a quick meditation strategy, whereas another day, I may need a hype man. Another day, I may need a refresher on brain breaks to give my students when they lose focus. How can these things be accessible to meet my needs at any given moment? Is there a playlist of quotes, activities, songs, or bite-sized PD to just give me that nudge, that boost?

It reminds me of the common phrase "they could have just sent that in an email." There are some teachers who need a quick bullet list of the important information, whereas some teachers need to be face to face. I believe this is one thing we learned that can take place and still be effective after COVID.

The key to all of this is knowing that administration may not get it right for everyone, but I believe it is a great stride in the right direction. Getting to know your staff just a bit more can really be the difference between striving to be a great school and being a great school.

A FINAL WORD ON DIFFERENTIATION FOR STAFF

Easy is easy, and difficult is difficult; there's no two ways around those facts. When we resist the temptation to not only make things easy for ourselves but to assume that everyone needs everything we put out, we find it much more effective to personalize our educational program. A few of the most basic needs of people are to be seen, valued, and heard. When we move from a one-size-fits-all model in teaching, we find that students are more engaged, and their needs are met at a more effective level. We should be doing the same for our staff as we plan professional development and create programs to improve our schools.

When we see our staff as a monolithic "thing," we don't see the individual personalities, strengths, and talents that make up the group. By considering how these elements coalesce into the greater being, we live what we expect for our students. We never find true educational success by aiming for the big middle of the group. Considering the needs of those ahead of the curve pulls us all up. Addressing the deficits of those who are behind the curve pushes us to ensure we are all headed in the same, upward direction. We need to take the time to plan for varying adult needs as we do our work. If our goal is to retain staff, it is always in our best interest to know them and work with them toward building their strengths within our organization. People who are seen in this light will surely want to stay and continue to grow with us!

CHAPTER 6
MAKE ROOM FOR REAL-LIFE STUFF
Consider the Lives of Your Staff Outside of School

*"Work-life balance is a real challenge;
if you are dedicated to work, chances are
you are not 'Daddycated' enough,
and vice-versa."*
~Vinay Goya

CREATING A BALANCE BETWEEN WORK AND LIFE CREATES STRESS THAT OFTEN CAUSES TEACHERS TO LEAVE

When I got my first teaching job, I was beyond excited. Part of the excitement was that I was going on an adventure. I grew up in Brooklyn, New York, and went to college in Oswego, New York. All my family was in the NYC metro area. However, my first teaching job took me to Houston, Texas, 1,600 miles from everyone I knew and was related to. As a 21-year-old young man, this was a terrific opportunity to see and experience a different part of the country, meet new people, and develop strong independence away from the safety of the family.

Fast forward this story to four years later. I moved to San Antonio and met my future wife. Four years after that we had the first of our three children. My wife's family is from Iowa and she also had nobody related to her in San Antonio. As a teacher and administrator, we were fortunate to have a generous amount of time off to take care of our first child, and 18 months later our second. We had great day-care providers who helped us devote time to work. We didn't have the option to drop our kids off at grandma's to run errands or go on dates, so we took them with us pretty much everywhere. They became great travelers too as we would go on long car trips to visit family "up north."

The downside of this arrangement was that we also did not have backup people for times when the kids were ill, daycare was closed, or doctor appointments were scheduled during the day. Going to the grocery store meant finding a cart with two seats and hauling groceries and kids around the store, parking lot, and back home. A few years later when child #3 came along, this work was compounded. I am not complaining about this, by the way. It was how it was, and we made some great memories doing some ordinary things. The point of this is that life was made a little bit easier because I had some flexibility, and my wife worked at a school that understood that sometimes life happened, and you had to be flexible at work.

I contrast my story to ones I've heard from educators I've known who tell a different tale. Stories of weekly meetings that went hours past work time; often right up to the time teachers had to pick up children from daycare. In the extreme, this type of disregard for people's lives can have a devastating effect on family dynamics and mental health. I know a school employee who was driven to therapy by the demands of a principal who didn't understand that in order to be a good employee she also had to be a good mother, wife, family member, and friend outside of work. Naturally, she left the toxic environment of the school where she was working. It was truly a loss for the students and community she served.

CREATE AN ENVIRONMENT THAT FACILITATES WORK-LIFE BALANCE

So much to do and so little time. We've all said this or at least thought it at some point in our lives. In education, this is even more true. There is a deceptive fallacy that exists in the public that school people work 9 months out of the year and put in a regular 8-hour day. To think all that needs to be done gets done in that amount of time is unrealistic. When you consider the active nature of what teachers do in a day and the amount of documentation their work produces, it's clear that teachers work far longer than their contracted hours. The result of this is a longer than typical workday using personal time to complete tasks.

For the most part, teachers understand this when they enter the profession. They know they will often sacrifice evenings for planning, grading, attending functions, and coaching. Knowing this, however, does not negate the fact that teachers have real lives outside of school that need to be lived. If we want to attract and keep great teachers, we need to create an environment where work-life balance can happen successfully.

How Do I Begin Creating Work-Life Balance for Staff?

The strategies in this chapter are both simple and difficult. Knowing that the work of a school does not just happen between the stated working hours of staff members, you need to be aware of the fact that anything that goes beyond their working hours is taking time from somewhere else. The mindset of the leader here needs to be on creating conveniences for staff and truly considering and honoring their lives outside of school. When you consider what we all have to do to keep ourselves and our families functioning, you can begin to think of ways that we can make our schools family-friendly.

Be as flexible as possible with time for life events. There are so many elements to running a household that can only be done during school hours. While over the years many businesses have moved to extended hours, there are still things that happen during the school day. If you have ever had a pet, a dental emergency, had blood drawn, or closed on a house (among a thousand other events) you know these things are rarely scheduled in the evening or on a weekend. Having been a school person most of my adult life, I sometimes forget that not everyone works our hours or follows our calendars.

One easy thing you can do for your staff is to create a procedure that will allow people to take up to 90 minutes during the day on occasion to run an errand without having to take personal time off. In one of my schools I gave each staff member two cards redeemable for this time and they could use them as they saw fit. Eventually, this evolved into me simply asking staff members to request the time as they needed it. If I could cover the time myself, with office staff, or volunteers the request was granted. Most often this time was used in the morning to come in late after having blood drawn, but it was also used to run to a child's school to see a program, to drop off a pet at the veterinarian's office, or to run to the bank to sign papers.

Connect with community resources to provide service at school. My first principalship was in a small town, and there was an auto repair shop that serviced many of our staff members' vehicles. I had a conversation with the owner, and he offered to provide a service to our staff members where he would pick up their vehicle from the school parking lot, perform the services, and then return the vehicle to the lot. All the staff member had to do was make the appointment and leave their keys at the front desk. This was a popular service, and it really helped our staff members save time they would have spent after school hours and on weekends. At another school, I had a local dry cleaner add our school to their pickup route. Staff members could bring their cleaning in bags provided by the dry cleaner, and the items would be picked up and delivered back to school when they were done. You can imagine this type of convenience benefited our staff members and also the businesses themselves!

Be creative with who you reach out to for staff convenience ideas. Call a few local businesses, and see if they would be willing to partner with your school to serve your staff. Check with the local oil change facility, call the grocery store to see if they can deliver to your school, for example. At one of my schools, we had a large chest freezer, and a company that made home deliveries of frozen foods would deliver items to that freezer to help staff who were not home during the day. There was a mobile auto brakes service who did that work in our school parking lot for those who needed it. A local fast food restaurant took group orders and brought a temperature controlled cooler to deliver meal orders that staff used not only for lunch but often to save a trip on their way home in the evening.

Allow staff to bring their children (and pets) to work! In my area there are several different school districts and each has a slightly different school calendar. Sometimes, there are student holidays and staff professional development days that don't align exactly. It is a good idea to allow staff members to bring their children to school with them on those days if they don't have alternate plans for childcare. There are so many benefits to allowing this! Students get to know their teacher's families which help develop the relationships between them to an even higher level. Staff members do not have to miss days of work to supervise their child and they are at ease knowing their child is safe and cared for. It also lets the child see where their parent or guardian works and gives them a glimpse into their "other life."

I had a new teacher tell me how much she appreciated that I allowed her daughter to spend a couple of days with her at work when we had alternate weeks for spring break. She expressed relief that she did not have to use her personal days (and as a new teacher she would not have many banked at that point). But she also commented on the fact that she felt even more connected to our school because it was clear that we put family first. I had a similar experience with a teacher a few years ago who needed that same consideration for her new puppy.

The only caveat to this suggestion is to check if your district has a policy on bringing family members or animals to school. In my experience, this is rarely, if ever, stated. It certainly requires additional thought and consideration of things like liability and allergies for example. However, if this is done on a very occasional basis and helps a staff member connect to your school, the rewards can be great!

Consider balance from another perspective. One of the most important lessons I learned as a school administrator is that what worked for me and what I considered best practices were not always the same for everyone. A great example is the fact that I didn't typically go to work on weekends or holidays. My expectation was that staff members would spend their non-work time with their families. While I was always happy to remotely turn off the alarm at the school, I often chided an employee that was working on a Sunday and told them they should be home on their sofa or out doing something fun. What I learned over the years was that for some staff members the time they spent working on a Sunday in the cool and quiet was essential for their wellbeing. One of my staff members used her Sunday afternoon in the classroom to fully prepare lesson materials for the week ahead. That time at school made her feel much less anxious and unprepared for the coming week. If you have a policy for building access, review it now, and consider allowing people the chance to work when they prefer outside of regular school hours. Ask your staff what they need for access, and make it happen.

I have learned that work-life balance for me is not the same as work-life balance for everyone else. When we learn to look at the needs and styles of others, we find that our role as administrators is to allow them to work the way they work best, not necessarily the way we work best. And by allowing ourselves to see the balance from their perspective we can be more effective at making our schools a place that meets their needs.

A PERSPECTIVE FROM THE FIELD

Dr. Pedro J. Cabrera, MJE, Professor of Communication and Journalism, Texas

First-year-teacher me was a mess, but weren't we all? I felt this need to prove myself and impress on all levels, as if I was the one getting graded in the end. I would take 120 spiral notebooks home with me on a Friday night in order to look over each and every one of them. My car, which was still the car I struggled forward with in college (missing front light and all), became the student work transport mobile. Rather than focus on my mental health and thriving relationships on a Friday night in the big city, I was head down and overwhelmed with grading and spirals.

It took an assistant principal to stop me as I was walking in on a Monday morning, carrying a pile of notebooks in my arms that rose to my chin, to tell me, "Don't do that again." Confused and thinking I was in trouble, I responded, "What do you mean, sir?"

"Spend your weekends with your family and friends," he responded. "Find ways to grade during the work day. Focus on the important things that matter on your off time."

That was my ah-ha moment. I was doing too much. Sadly, that is what teachers are wired to do – constantly reach the limit for others and, eventually, reach their own limit of exhaustion, which then increases the likelihood of thinking about leaving the profession. Thankfully, my personality is resilient – I needed to figure out a way to manage all-things-teaching, and it was because my assistant principal saw a bad trait beginning to develop.

However, having been in education for over a decade, I don't remember having time management and work management as a class or distinct professional development. As a whole, the perception may be that we teach teachers how to create a lesson and teach children, but we don't teach them how to manage the day-to-day responsibilities of being a teacher. Then, it becomes fight or flight, thrown into the deep end to tread water.

It is incredibly vital to provide teachers with tools and resources to schedule and plan, delegate and prioritize. It is also important for leaders to do the same thing – requiring teachers to jump without having a plan in place is malpractice and stressful for those who are simply trying to tread water.

A STEP-BY-STEP GUIDE TO CREATING A CULTURE OF WORK-LIFE BALANCE

STEP 1 - **Create opportunities for staff to take care of business**

Our school day ran from 7:00 AM-3:15 PM for most staff members. Unfortunately, this was also the time that the "real world" ran in many instances. If at all possible, allow staff members to take care of personal business for a reasonable amount of time during the school day. This could mean having a system for covering classes and duties so they can get things done. I was asked recently if a staff member could leave at 2:00 to get her daughter to the dentist. The teacher told me she would take a half-day off if I needed her to do that instead. I told her we would cover the class for dismissal (2:55 PM for us) so she could run this errand. This saves on trying to get a substitute for a half-day and also has the teacher in the class for a great majority of the day as well. This type of flexibility helps her and also reinforces the culture of family-first in our school. It's a win-win for all of us!

STEP 2 - Use your resources

Most of our communities have service-oriented businesses that could potentially serve our school staff while building their customer base. If we look for the type of services our staff would need, we could create connections with these businesses to provide their services to the school community. This creates a kind of symbiotic relationship that benefits both the school and the community we serve. One great example was when we had a community member who was building her yoga business. She offered to lead a few complimentary weekly classes for our staff to both provide a much-needed service toward their self-care goals while also promoting her services which could result in people signing up for more classes.

When we think about what people need, we can look for those connections and help create situations where our staff have a value-added experience in our schools. This is a key to helping build a culture where people want to stay.

STEP 3 - Make your school a family-friendly space

Schools are not like factories. The essence of our work is to develop people at different stages of their lives in age-appropriate facilities. School is also where most of our adults spend most of their days. So, when we create working spaces that consider and celebrate the fact that our people have a life outside school, we go a long way to build the culture to retain them. Not only the examples of allowing for staff to bring their children to school but also encouraging their families to be part of school activities and events. Some of the best festivals and programs we had at our school had staff member families running booths, passing out programs, and helping with activities. This helps not only create positive connections to the school but also the positive image of the school to those families.

In my practice as an elementary school leader, I have found that creating family-friendly alternatives has been consistently appreciated by staff members. As long as your school district policy doesn't prohibit this, you can provide this perk at no cost, but with a ton of goodwill earned!

STEP 4 - Really know what your staff needs

When I was a new assistant principal, I had a teacher at my school that was floundering. He had almost no classroom management routines, and his class was chaotic and unpleasant. He and I both knew it wasn't working for him or the students in his classroom. I had the great idea to take him to visit a teacher I had observed at another school who was an absolute master at routines and procedures. Her classroom ran efficiently and was a place of joy and learning. I took the teacher to that classroom to visit with confidence that he would absorb what she was doing and be able to implement the same things in his classroom.

What I didn't realize is that as a newer teacher he would be overwhelmed with all the pieces she had going on in her classroom. It was like drinking water from a firehose when we went to visit. He couldn't latch on to any of the procedures, nor could he understand how they were implemented. From this experience, I learned that even though I often could see what someone might need, it only mattered if they saw the need. My role was to listen more and tell less. I needed to guide the discussion to a place where he could see and understand what he needed, then help him find a way to meet the needs.

Whenever you think that your teachers need more school events, more games at PD sessions, more reflection, more time, more food, or more pushing, take the time to stop yourself and look at things from their perspective. Talk to people, observe what they're feeling, and listen as they tell you (often in shrouded language) what they really need. Then, find ways to make it happen.

A PERSPECTIVE FROM THE FIELD

Jacki Mjoen - Seventh Grade Math Teacher, Illinois

During my fourth year teaching I never expected the words "brain tumor" to be my reality. But there it was, as real as my pencil supply running low in my seventh grade math classroom.

In July 2022, I was diagnosed with stage two glioma… aka brain cancer. I didn't realize the extent to which I would need the support of my admin until then. They have always supported me as an educator and welcomed new ideas, but this just got personal and real. My admin stepped right into the gap without hesitation. Between finding sub coverage, frequent check-ins, and extra chocolate in my mailbox, their support gave me permission to practice what I encourage in my classroom... come as you are. This was exactly what I needed on the days when showing up for my middle schoolers felt like more than what I had capacity for. Their support went beyond just feeling seen, I was known. I was no longer just a teacher, I was a teacher battling cancer.

I would be lying to myself if I didn't think this would impact my ability to show up for my kids. Teachers are "on" from the first bell to the last. Should I keep this information from the kids? Again, I was forced to face the motto I stood behind in my classroom... come as you are. I decided to tell my seventh graders the news, and it was the best thing I could have done. I was overwhelmed with grace, love, and encouraging emails I will be saving forever. During my radiation treatment, the brain fog was real. I would find myself writing incorrect numbers on the board, and I could hear the awkward silence behind me. I would turn to the kids in confusion, they would smile, and someone would lovingly say, "it's just the radiation Mrs. Mjoen." It was at that moment I felt the value of practicing the transparency I hope for with the kids. I had now given my kids permission to fully know me.

Whether we like it or not, our outside lives influence our work lives. Our job requires us to extend all of ourselves for the needs of kids. Whoever said we needed to do it alone? Vulnerability is the key to making room for real-life stuff.

WHAT COULD POSSIBLY GO WRONG?

If you were dedicated you would not complain.

There is always a risk when lines are blurry. On social media, I often read about school employees who complain that their administration does not take into account or respect their time. Meetings are when meetings are. There are so many required elements that happen outside of traditional work hours and so frequently, that teachers feel resentful of the time encroachment. In these posts, teachers often relate that they are made to feel as if they are not dedicated enough to the school and their students if they can't/won't/don't want to participate. We've got to stop this and find a workable solution.

Dedication to one's self, family, or community does not translate into a lack of dedication to their school or students. It's unrealistic to say that everything teachers do can be done completely during their contracted work hours. However, we as administrators need to understand that when we routinely expect people to work beyond their time to do things that could be done during their day, we are taking away from their "real life" time. The middle ground lies in communication with staff members and sensitivity to their needs, especially at certain times of the year. Considering our calendars and adjusting to provide more time during contracted hours goes a long way to overcoming pushback to working beyond hours on an occasional basis.

I don't have the staff to cover people's appointments.
Or maybe you do... This is a common concern when considering how to cover classes and duties for people who occasionally need about 90 minutes or so to take care of a personal errand during school hours. When you think about how to do this, you often need to be creative about what and where things happen. As long as this doesn't happen every day, you can often provide coverage with administrative, counseling, or office staff for that amount of time depending on what you have available. This means we all have to be flexible and understand that sometimes we will need to be somewhere we didn't intend to be when the day begins or ends. During the pandemic we often found ourselves substituting and creatively covering classes due to a severe shortage of substitute teachers. While this was done out of necessity, we could also consider that on an occasional basis we can provide the same coverage to each other to prevent absences so people can get their personal business accomplished.

I will put one caveat on this bit of pushback. If you find that you have people who overuse this privilege you may have to create some limits. In my experience, this does not happen frequently, but it does happen. Many years ago I had an employee that was consistently 5-10 minutes late to work. I found out that it was because as a single mother with children, she was finding it difficult to get everyone ready to go, then drop off kids at two different schools. I worked with her to adjust her schedule so she could start 15 minutes later and end 15 minutes later in the afternoon. This worked beautifully until it didn't. As time went on I discovered that she was now arriving 5-10 minutes late even on the new schedule. We ended up having a more focused discussion on the importance of being on time. The lesson to me was to try to truly discern needs from habits and act accordingly.

Our school (or District) doesn't allow employee's children (or pets) at work.

When considering this bit of pushback it's important to understand whether there is actually a written policy regarding this practice, or if it's just "what we've done around here." I find that in cases such as this there is often nothing in the policy that forbids this specifically. There are often vague statements regarding liability that are not often followed by specific details. The best advice for overcoming this bit of pushback is to simply check your school or district policy before granting permission for a staff member's child to come to school with them.

If your district does have a specific policy that forbids this practice, it might be a good time to consider how to go about modifying the policy to suit the current needs of your staff. Perhaps there was (or is) a good reason to have such a policy, but in my many years of educational leadership in several school districts, I have not seen this situation cause any issues. On the contrary, there was an increase in staff attendance and satisfaction when staff members were allowed to bring their children on a limited basis. It is a win-win for both the staff member and the school.

Pets might be a different animal altogether (pun intended). There are likely no written policies for this in your school district, but there can be issues with student allergies, potential behavioral concerns, or student fear of certain pets. This may be a more extreme staff perk, but on a case-by-case basis, if you can make it work you should!

CREATING A CULTURE OF WORK-LIFE BALANCE IN REAL LIFE

When you have been in education as long as I have you should never think you've heard it all. I promise you there is always something you're going to be asked that you haven't heard before. That being said, here are two examples of this concept in action.

I hired a new Pre-Kindergarten teacher who was amazing in every way. She knew her stuff, built incredible relationships, and was loved by staff, students, and families alike. She had three children of her own in various stages of growing up. Her youngest was in elementary school and went to a different school in a different school district.

At one point, the teacher had a situation where her daughter had a different spring break than ours. She had childcare worked out for most of the break, but there was an issue the last two days. She was thinking she was going to have to take the days off to be home. She mentioned this to me, and I suggested that if she wanted to bring her daughter to work and not use her leave days, she was welcome to do so. The teacher was relieved to say the least. Being new to the district, she did not have a large bank of leave to draw from, and with three kids, there were always things that required days off.

Her daughter had an amazing time at school. She helped her mom with her class and more importantly got to see her mom in a different role. This outcome was a definite win-

win for all of us. The teacher was relieved that she could come to work and also care for her child. The students got to know a little bit more about their teacher as a person. The daughter got to see how amazing her mother was as a teaching professional. It also built a stronger bond between the mom and the school. The school is not just a place to go to work, but a place that values family.

Another story that validates my initial comment about something new always happening is from three years ago. One of my fifth-grade teachers acquired a fantastic new dachshund puppy. Her concern was that she would be gone for long days during the initial training and socialization period. She knew it was a long shot, but she asked me if she could bring the crated puppy to school and tend to his needs during her planning and lunch periods. She assured me the puppy would not distract the students from what they needed to do during the day.

My initial reaction was that this might not be a great idea. There are issues that exist when you co-mingle kids and animals. However, I decided that rather than just outright say no, we could give it a try as long as she informed her families and addressed any objections they might have. Once she got that approved, the pup began to visit the class daily.

The original idea was that this arrangement would last for up to three weeks. What ended up happening was that he became something of a class and school mascot. He was a very well-behaved dog, and he got the advantage of socialization from his interactions with the students. While this benefited him it also was a benefit to the students.

They learned about proper dog care, had lessons in compassion and care, and developed a stronger bond with their teacher because as in the example above, they got to know her better as a person.

A PERSPECTIVE FROM THE FIELD

Tim Stephenson, Secondary Science Teacher, British Columbia, Canada

Ah yes, the age-old question: "Do teachers actually have a life outside of school?" Well, it turns out that they do, and from what I've seen, it raises an interesting dilemma that should be addressed.

You see, teacher commitments outside of school are often dealt with by leaving the building as quickly after the bell as possible. This practice conflicts with one of my personal tenets of successful teaching which is that after school time is when the magic happens! Coaching, clubs, and special projects are just the beginning of what it truly means to be a teacher. But how does one grapple with these conflicts when the teacher's own children need to be picked up, or driven somewhere, or personal activities need to be attended to?

It's not a question with an easy answer, and certainly there should never be judgment placed upon anyone who is trying to manage the stresses of teaching AND the responsibilities of life. But is that the reason why teachers leaving do so quickly and sometimes out the backdoor where they may go undetected? How can the realities of work-life balance coexist peacefully with the perception that school should come first?

I believe Marty has shown that there are solutions to this dilemma. It starts with school leadership truly making an effort to know the staff and their individual needs and situations. A happy staff is one that is acknowledged for doing a great job in the classroom while at the same time acknowledged for their efforts away from school. Bringing in dry cleaners and oil changes to the school is awesome. As is allowing pets and teachers' children into the school.

In my school, we hold a staff social once per month called the BBB. This stands for Birthdays and Boasts Bash! The admin team pays for coffee, tea and snacks, and staff gather to be celebrated for their work outside of school. Perhaps they ran a marathon, got married, completed a home renovation, sank a hole-in-one, or had a birthday. All these things get acknowledged and each person receives a rose for their efforts or their birthday. Staff members nominate their colleagues as they hear about these achievements and milestones.

The individual teacher's stage of life and the fact that we all live within the same 24-hour time limit means that we will all contribute to the school what we can and when we can. The school is a community, and school is a "people business." This dynamic equilibrium will shift in harmony the more we see the needs of the people and respect the place in life they are at.

A FINAL WORD ABOUT A CULTURE OF WORK-LIFE BALANCE

True balance is a tricky thing. In our culture, there is a strong push to make work a priority, and this can be particularly challenging for those of us in education. We pour from ourselves on a daily basis to enrich others and often don't have much more to give our families and communities. Teachers will often say that this is the reason they leave a place or even the profession. It is vital for school leaders to look at work-life balance situations and do what we can to alleviate the pressures for teachers so they can not only stay in our schools but can be effective as people outside school. When that balance occurs we enhance not just the schools but the communities we live in and serve.

There are so many potential limitations that can stop us from being as family-friendly to our people as we'd like. The easy solution would be to put a sharp separation between work life and home life. Often this leads to an initial inclination to say no to any requests that blend the two worlds. My advice is to curb that inclination. When we look for doable solutions that benefit both our schools and our people, we create situations that draw people to us and keep them coming back!

CONCLUSION

*"School culture is the set of norms,
values and beliefs, rituals and ceremonies,
symbols and stories that make up
the 'persona' of the school."*
~Terrence Deal and Kent Peterson

The summer I was 15, I worked in the factory where my dad worked in the Garment District in New York City. My job was in the stockroom. I received printed orders for the handbags that were manufactured in the factory, and I picked them from shelves and boxed them up to be sent to stores around the country. That job was a job. While I had co-workers, most of us worked solo and just got the orders filled. Our interactions were not essential to what we did, though it was nice to have others around to interact with during the day and not have to eat lunch alone.

Education is a whole other type of career. When I read the quote at the beginning of this section, it reminds me that school is more than books, technology, playground equipment, whiteboards, curriculum, and report cards. While there is assuredly a science to education, there is also an art, and a school culture can be best described as the visualization of that art.

People want to be connected and feel like they are seen, valued, and heard in an organization. When that doesn't happen people often search for another organization where these needs can be met. It is our duty and a significant part of our role as school administrators and teachers to sustain a culture where people not only want to belong, but encourage others to belong as well.

As you read, I hope you found some ideas and action steps to nurture your school culture into one that makes people want to stay. By sustaining a culture of excellence for the people that come to our schools every day, we affirm the fact that our school is the place to be. An investment in building an excellent culture will reap impressive gains both academically and socially with all members of your school community.

I wish you much success on your journey toward sustaining excellence!

ACKNOWLEDGEMENTS

I call this book my elephant baby. It has been gestating for a REALLY long time in my head, in my notes, and in my communication with lots of colleagues and friends over a very long period of time. I'm so excited that this calf is finally born! While I'd like to think I did this all by myself, there are so many people who have helped bring this book to its current form.

First and foremost, I would like to thank Joy Scott Ressler for providing the initial impetus to start putting these thoughts into written words. Without your support and enthusiasm, this book may never have made it to the published page. I'd also like to thank Jen Z. Marshall for your ideas, support, and editing when this book was gestating.

To Ryan Scott for your encouragement and support as I began putting the words to paper. I am deeply grateful. Your positive energy helped shape this project into what it is today.

To the teachers and administrators who worked with me and have become school leaders yourselves. Denise Boehme, Terry Combs, Daniel Martinez, Joshua Ellis, Michelle Allen, Alma Neira, Julie Meneses, Cindy Cavazos Taylor, Kristi Ann Villanueva, Kevin Hans, Charlotte Turlington, Aimee Tijerina-Lara, Dawn Van Damme, Natasha Williams, Tom Ilgenfritz, and others. I am so proud of you always, and hope you have taken a few of the great things we did together and spread them to your new spaces!

I would also like to extend my thanks to the incredible educators from all over the country who agreed to provide Voices from the Field pieces for this book. Your words make a significant impact in this work. Thanks for not only agreeing to read chapters, but for finding the places where our thoughts and experiences intersected.

Special thanks go to the hundreds of colleagues I had the honor of teaching alongside and leading alongside during my fabulous 40-year career in education. Every time I thought I was in a perfect situation, I found out I was correct because of the devotion, dedication, and love I found in my schools and among my colleagues. I always had long commutes to work, and I never regretted that. My enthusiasm for showing up every day was directly due to the fact that I loved coming to work in places where people wanted everything good for our kids and communities.

To my network of supportive educators around the country and around the world, your encouragement has meant the world to me. Thank you for pouring into me and giving me perspectives from other places. I appreciate how many of you agreed to share yourselves on my podcast and/or serving as Guest Readers from around the world!

Thanks to the contributions of Dr. Jeff Springer and Dr. Daryl Porter to this work and to my success at staying focused, sane, and supported while I wrote this book.

Brian Miller, if you don't know this already, my goal is still to be half the writer you are.

Thanks to my sisters, Donna, Rena, and Sheila for making my crib the Principal's Office when they were playing school as children. You clearly imprinted this life onto me and I'm forever grateful!

Finally, I owe a huge debt of gratitude to Darrin and Jess Peppard from Road to Awesome for their belief that this topic needed to be addressed in education. Your commitment and belief in me made this book possible, and I cannot thank you enough.

Thank you all for being part of this journey.

ABOUT THE AUTHOR

Martin Silverman is a father, grandfather, husband, and long-time educator in beautiful San Antonio, Texas. He has been committed to providing the best educational experience for the students and families at Salinas Elementary School where he recently retired as principal. Martin has worked as a teacher and administrator in urban, suburban, and rural districts. His interests are creating and nurturing school culture, providing enriching experiences for students and families, and developing future teachers and administrators. As a former bilingual teacher and administrator, Martin is committed to providing ELL students with quality programs to develop their unique skills. He hosts a podcast called *The Second Question*, which highlights educators and provides them a forum to discuss ideas and honor the teachers who have influenced their lives.

Work with Martin Silverman
Martin Silverman is a veteran educator, mentor, speaker, consultant, and coach. He specializes in building school culture, improving communication, early childhood educational success, and incorporating special programs to ensure all students succeed. Please visit his website (mrsilverman.com) for more information on him and how to contact him to work with you and your school.

MORE BOOKS FROM ROAD TO AWESOME

Taking the Leap: A Field Guide for Aspiring School Leaders by Robert F. Breyer

Transform: Techy Notes to Make Learning Sticky by Debbie Tannenbaum

Becoming Principal: A Leadership Journey & The Story of School Community by Dr. Jeff Prickett

Elevate Your Vibe: Action Planning with Purpose by Lisa Toebben

#OwnYourEpic: Leadership Lessons in Owning Your Voice and Your Story by Dr. Jay Dostal

The Design Thinking, Entrepreneurial, Visionary Planning Leader: A Practical guide for Thriving in Ambiguity by Dr. Michael Nagler

Becoming the Change: Five Essential Elements to Being Your Best Self by Dan Wolfe

inspired: moments that matter by Melissa Wright

Foundations of Instructional Coaching: Impact People, Improve Instruction, Increase Success by Ashley Hubner

Out of the Trenches: Stories of Resilient Educators
by Dana Goodier

Principled Leader
by Bobby Pollicino

Road to Awesome: The Journey of a Leader
by Darrin Peppard

When Calling Parents Isn't Your Calling: A teacher's guide to communicating with all parents
by Crystal Frommert

Struggle to Strength: Finding the Ingredients to Your Secret Sauce
by Kip Shubert

Guiding Transformational Change in Education
by Kristina V. Mattis

Be the Cause: An Educator's Guide to EFFECTive Instruction
by Josh Korb

Called to Empower
by Coach Kurt Hines

The Blueprint: Survive and Thrive as a School Administrator
by Todd M. Bloomer

CHILDREN'S BOOKS FROM ROAD TO AWESOME

Road to Awesome A Journey for Kids
by Jillian DuBois and Darrin M. Peppard

Emersyn Blake and the Spotted Salamander
by Kim Collazo

Theodore Edward Makes a New Friend
by Alyssa Schmidt

I'm Autistic and I'm Awesome
by Derek Danziger

Emersyn Blake and the Stalked Jellyfish
by Kim Collazo

Birdie & Mipps
by Barbara Gruener

www.ingramcontent.com/pod-product-compliance
Lightning Source LLC
Chambersburg PA
CBHW060348190426
43201CB00043B/1768